AWS CERTIFIED CLOUD PRACTITIONER STUDY GUIDE:

The Ultimate Cheat Sheet Practice Exam Questions With Answers & Detailed Explanations For The Latest CLF-01 Exam

Barry Adams

© Copyright 2020 - All rights reserved.

The content contained within this book may not be reproduced, duplicated or transmitted without direct written permission from the author or the publisher. Under no circumstances will any blame or legal responsibility be held against the publisher, or author, for any damages, reparation, or monetary loss due to the information contained within this book. Either directly or indirectly.

Legal Notice:

This book is copyright protected. This book is only for personal use. You cannot amend, distribute, sell, use, quote or paraphrase any part, or the content within this book, without the consent of the author or publisher.

Disclaimer Notice:

Please note the information contained within this document is for educational and entertainment purposes only. All effort has been executed to present accurate, up to date, and reliable, complete information. No warranties of any kind are declared or implied. Readers acknowledge that the author is not engaging in the rendering of legal, financial, medical or professional advice. The content within this book has been derived from various sources. Please consult a licensed professional before attempting any techniques outlined in this book.

By reading this document, the reader agrees that under no circumstances is the author responsible for any losses, direct or indirect, which are incurred as a result of the use of information contained within this document, including, but not limited to, errors, omissions, or inaccuracies.

TABLE OF CONTENTS

INTRODUCTION: 6
- DOMAIN 1: CLOUD CONCEPTS 11
- DOMAIN 2: SECURITY AND COMPLIANCE 11
- DOMAIN 3: TECHNOLOGY 11
- DOMAIN 4: BILLING AND PRICING 12

CHAPTER 1: CLOUD CONCEPTS 14
- WHAT IS CLOUD COMPUTING? 14
- DEPLOYMENT MODELS 16
- REVIEW QUESTIONS 17

CHAPTER 2: SECURITY 28
- BENEFITS OF AWS SECURITY 29
- THE SHARED RESPONSIBILITY MODEL 30
- MONITORING AND LOGGING FEATURES 32
- IDENTIFY AND ACCESS MANAGEMENT. 32
- REVIEW QUESTIONS 34

CHAPTER 3: TECHNOLOGY 43
- AWS ORGANIZATION AND ACCOUNTS 43
- AWS CORE SERVICES 44
- DATABASE SERVICES 44
- AWS COMPUTING 46
- AWS STORAGE SERVICES 48
- AWS LOGGING SERVICES 49
- REVIEW QUESTIONS 51

CHAPTER 4: BILLING AND PRICING 62
- RELIABILITY DESIGN PRINCIPLES 62
- AWS TRUSTED ADVISOR 63
- AWS RELIABILITY FAILURE MANAGEMENT SERVICES 65
- BACKUP AND RESTORE 66
- PILOT LIGHT ARCHITECTURE 67
- FULLY WORKING LOW-CAPACITY STANDBY ARCHITECTURE 67
- RELIABILITY BEST PRACTICES 68
- REVIEW QUESTIONS 68

CHAPTER 5: AWS SERVICES 78
- EXECUTION EFFICIENCY 79
- THE STANDARD FOR EXECUTION: 79
- DEMOCRATIZE CUTTING EDGE INNOVATIONS: 79
- PLAN PRINCIPLES OF COST IMPROVEMENT IN THE CLOUD: 81
- CONSUMPTION AWARENESS 83

UPGRADING OVER TIME..84
CHAPTER 6: HOW TO SECURE YOUR AWS RESOURCES 86
CREATING A STRONG PASSWORD FOR YOUR ACCOUNT IN THE
CLOUD 86
USING A GROUP E-MAIL ALIAS...87
ENABLE OR APPLY MULTI-FACTOR AUTHENTICATION PROCESS
....87
DAILY ACCOUNT ACCESS REQUIRES YOU TO SETUP GROUPS,
USERS, AND ROLES. 88
DELETE OR REMOVE YOUR ACCOUNT'S ACCESS KEYS.................. 88
IDENTITY AND ACCESSIBILITY MANAGEMENT IN AWS.................89
HOW IDENTITY AND ACCESSIBILITY MANAGEMENT WORKS......89
BEST PRACTICES FOR IDENTITY AND ACCESSIBILITY
MANAGEMENT IN AWS 90
USE CASES FOR IAM IN AMAZON WEB SERVICES 90
AUTHENTICATION PROCESSES... 91
THE ROLES OF USER GROUPS IN AWS 92

CONCLUSION 96
ANSWERS TO REVIEW QUESTIONS 100
CLOUD CONCEPTS...100
SECURITY..120
TECHNOLOGY 130
BILLING AND PRICING 146

Introduction:

I am addicted to certification! I have been receiving I.T. certifications for over 18 years, have passed 50+ exams during this period, and have failed only twice for one exam. I will explain how to pass the AWS certification exams the first time.

The key to passing the AWS certification exams is simply preparing correctly. Preparation includes the following five steps that I will explain in this post:

- Practice (practice)

- Training (mainly online video)

- Theory (read)

- Practical questions

- Take the test

Many companies also sell different resources to prepare you for exams. Still, the material's quality can vary widely, so it's worth paying attention to what you use.

BACKGROUND OF THE INVESTIGATION

Many people who take these exams have the necessary computer skills. It may be much more difficult for you if you are a newcomer and cannot distinguish a block from an object store or container virtual machine. That said, you don't need to have excellent skills in the underlying technologies that support AWS since cloud computing removes much of that complexity.

In the exam plan, AWS makes the following recommendations for AWS-specific knowledge and experience.

The exam recently changed the format this year. The following image shows the differences between the new and old form (this applies to all AWS certification exams at the corresponding level).

AWS technology is evolving incredibly fast, so I would recommend using the latest exam format if you start your studies now as it will better match the features available today. It is not as generous as the more incredible difficulty of some of the questions on the new exam. But don't be discouraged, the accompanying exams aren't too tricky, and you have plenty of resources to prepare.

STEP 1: IT ALL BEGINS WITH PRACTICE

One of the keys to learning technology is to play with it. Don't worry if you don't work with AWS. Not everyone can work with the technologies they study in a professional context, and indeed, I have passed many exams without real work experience.

AWS allows you to create an account for free, and the free tier will enable you to use specific AWS services for free.

The free tier offers many free services every month, including (among others):

Free AWS tier: It's a great way to gain experience, and you can take things out and take them apart without costing you a penny. It's amazing what you can do on the free tier for a whole year!

STEP 2: ONLINE VIDEO TRAINING

Online video training is an excellent tool. There are many AWS certification courses online that allow you to relax and absorb everything.

Classes can range from PowerPoint to highly lab-oriented, and this is where the problem of their isolated Use lies. Courses with a lot of content can be very dry and dull, and more practical terms will be light and will help you get ready to take the exam.

To make sure you pass the exam and gain hands-on experience on AWS for the first time, sign up for the latest AWS Certified cloud practitioner hands-on video training in digital cloud training.

STEP 3: THEORY

Some people find it boring, but there is no substitute for theory, and there is still plenty to read. I like to practice a lot of I.T. before getting caught up in the theoretical part that helps things make sense (and keeps it interesting). It is essential to keep practicing as you gain more knowledge: use it or lose it!

The AWS website contains a wealth of information, so you can use it pretty much if you want. There are books and e-books, too, but things are changing rapidly in the AWS world and are generally updated with time.

My strategy in learning theory is to take lots of notes. When I look at the online courses, I also pay attention to the essential facts. Having concise and summary training notes becomes invaluable when you try to remember thousands of points because you can come back to them at any time without having to read long articles. Try a digital note-taking tool like Microsoft OneNote or Evernote.

STEP 4: PRACTICAL QUESTION

Using high-quality, practical questions will help you understand the types of questions you may encounter during the exam and identify weaknesses.

However, the challenge is to find excellent quality practice questions. There have always been many exams on the Internet, and various companies have low-quality questions (which they generally copy between themselves).

Remember that AWS changes quickly, so questions must be current. I want to avoid common or expired problems!

I suggest that you test multiple times during your preparation, don't wait for the exam time. The practical questions should be considered both a learning tool and an assessment tool and should be used from the beginning.

STEP 5: EXAM TIME

Another key to my success in I.T. certification exams is that I have never booked the exam before. I am sure I am ready. You should receive 80 to 90% of the practical questions just before you think about booking.

The actual pass rate is much lower than this. Still, there will always be surprises during the day with technologies that you haven't covered enough during training.

Once you've trained, taken a course, viewed my training notes, and passed the training questions, you're ready to go. If you prepared well, you don't have to get crowded at the last minute, so get rid of all the stress and come back.

Try to read each question first and see the answers. You can develop talent for this and often quickly discover what the answer will be. Go back to the problem in detail and make sure you haven't forgotten anything before choosing.

Some questions are an objective, a multiple choice with multiple answers, and you may need to select "all that apply." Make sure you are not mistaken, as it is an easy mistake to make!

AWS certification exams are reasonably well written, so there are generally not many confusing questions. If you have prepared high-quality, practical questions to prepare yourself, you will need to be well equipped to handle everything. Good study and good luck with your exams!

Domain 1: Cloud Concepts 26%

Domain 2: Security and Compliance 25%

Domain 3: Technology 33%

Domain 4: Billing and Pricing 16%

TOTAL 100%

Domain 1: Cloud Concepts

1.1. Define the AWS Cloud and its value proposition

1.2 Identify aspects of AWS Cloud economics

1.3 List the different cloud architecture design principles

Domain 2: Security and Compliance

2.1 Define the AWS shared responsibility model

2.2 Define AWS Cloud security and compliance concepts

2.3 Identify AWS access management capabilities

2.4 Identify resources for security support

Domain 3: Technology

3.1 Define methods of deploying and operating in the AWS Cloud

3.2 Define the AWS global infrastructure

3.3 Identify the core AWS services

3.4 Identify resources for technology support

Domain 4: Billing and Pricing

4.1 Compare and contrast the various pricing models for AWS

4.2 Recognize the different account structures about AWS billing and pricing

4.3 Identify resources available for billing support

CHAPTER 1:

Cloud Concepts

Setting up your own data center is time-consuming and costly: skilled personnel must acquire and maintain. Also, you can never scale as needed. After all, your company should grow, and therefore your I.T. must always be one step ahead. For this reason, you often provide more resources than the employees currently need. After all, a functioning data center is vital for most companies. If it fails, the work stops. And nobody can afford that, so you have to spend too much rather than too little at the data center.

With cloud computing, you go a different way: Instead of purchasing, installing, and maintaining the technology yourself, you can use web services. In most cases, this form of modern outsourcing runs through a rental model. Capacities can be quickly booked in this way - and promptly when you need them.

What is Cloud Computing?

In principle, cloud computing is only a collective term: This describes the offer of hardware and software over the Internet. It does not specify the extent to which the services must be provided - from simple cloud storage, in which users receive storage capacity on remote servers in addition to their own hard disk space, to the infrastructure in the cloud, through which companies have complete data centers via the Internet Respectively.

Definition of cloud computing

On-demand self-service: It should be possible for users to independently request the required resources without having to contact an employee of the provider each time.

Broad Network Access: Access to cloud computing works over the Internet. No unusual techniques or protocols may be used. The Use of standardized methods ensures that all users have easy access to the service.

Resource pooling: The merging of several computing instances is the essential prerequisite for cloud computing. Such pools are usually used in the form of server farms to supply several users with computing power or storage capacity at the same time. It is rarely apparent to the customer which device he is using: The accommodations are allocated dynamically.

Rapid elasticity: The delivery of capacities has to be quick and needs-based. At best, automatisms are active that switch resources on or off without customers' or employees' help.

Measured Service: The Use of the cloud offer is monitored at all times. It creates more transparency for both the provider and the user.

Deployment Models

The deployment models describe the type of offer: Are instances reserved for only one user or company, or do you share the pool with other people? The deployment model results from the answer to this question.

Community Cloud: The Community Cloud works in a similar way to a private cloud, but with this model, several customers share a dedicated hardware instance. The users' users' composition is not chosen at random. Still, several customers - mostly from the same business area or with similar interests - come together in a targeted manner. The Community Cloud can also be managed either in a company or externally. The goal is to achieve savings compared to multiple private clouds. Public cloud: This type of provision corresponds to the basic idea behind a cloud. A server network is used together with the general public. Who uses which hardware is not visible to the user and cannot be determined by him.

Hybrid cloud: This is a hybrid of the two models of the private and public clouds. A company or a remote user decides to leave a specific part of the operation (e.g., security-related aspects) in the intimate environment and choose the public cloud for other details.

It is cloud computing.

You can also rent I.T. Most of these I.T. services providers are geographically distant. Hence, the data and applications are no longer on your company's local computer but in the cloud. It just means that your information is no longer stored directly with you, but away from the company center. And only you. The advantages are more flexibility, scalability, and low costs since there is no separate server structure. Do you think that is not the case with you? Not correct! As soon as you have an e-mail address on the Internet, enter your username and password there; you are a cloud provider user. Other examples would be:

- Dropbox

- Microsoft OneDrive

- Google Drive

- Amazon Drive

- iCloud

However, when choosing your "cloud provider," you should make sure that all relevant security regulations are met. By the way, the world's world's strictest security requirements apply in Germany, which is why many companies choose a cloud "Made in Germany."

REVIEW QUESTIONS

Question 1

Which items can be configured from within the VPC management console? (Select TWO.)

1. Regions

2. Load Balancing

3. Security Groups

4. Subnets

5. Auto Scaling

Question 2

Which benefit of the AWS Cloud eliminates the need for users to try estimating future infrastructure usage?

1. Economies of scale

2. Easy global deployments

3. Security of the AWS Cloud

4. The elasticity of the AWS Cloud

Question 3

Which AWS support plan should you use if you need a response time of < 15 minutes for a business-critical system failure?

1. Basic

2. Developer

3. Business

4. Enterprise

Question 4

Under the shared responsibility model, what are examples of shared controls? (Select TWO.)

1. Storage system patching
2. Physical and environmental
3. Patch management
4. Service and Communications Protection
5. Configuration management

Question 5

Which feature of AWS allows you to deploy a new application for which the requirements may change over time?

1. Elasticity
2. Fault tolerance
3. High availability
4. Disposable resources

Question 6

Which of the statements below is accurate regarding Amazon S3 buckets? (Select TWO.)

1. Bucket names must be unique regionally
2. Bucket names must be unique globally

3. Buckets are replicated globally

4. Buckets are region-specific

5. Buckets can contain other buckets

Question 7

The AWS global infrastructure is composed of? (Select TWO.)

1. Clusters

2. I.P. Subnets

3. Fault Zones

4. Availability Zones

5. Regions

Question 8

A company stores copies of backups on Amazon S3 and requires rapid access but low resiliency. Which storage class is optimized for these requirements?

1. Amazon S3 Glacier

2. Amazon S3 One Zone-Infrequent Access

3. Amazon S3 Standard

4. Amazon S3 Glacier Deep Archive

Question 9

What is the term for describing the action of automatically running scripts on Amazon EC2 instances when launched to install software?

1. Workflow Automation

2. Bootstrapping

3. Golden Images

4. Containerization

Question 10

Which service can be used for building and integrating loosely-coupled, distributed applications?

1. Amazon EFS

2. Amazon RDS

3. Amazon EBS

4. Amazon SNS

Question 11

Which AWS service allows you to connect to storage from on-premise servers using standard file protocols?

1. Amazon Glacier

2. Amazon EFS

3. Amazon EBS

4. Amazon S3

Question 12

Which service allows you to run code as functions without needing to provision or manage servers?

1. AWS Lambda
2. Amazon EC2
3. AWS CodeDeploy
4. Amazon EKS

Question 13

To transfer a website to one type of Cloud while its brochure is on another, which Cloud can be used?

A. Real Cloud

B. Private Cloud

C. Dynamic Cloud

D. Hybrid Cloud

Question 14

When public and private cloud services are mixed, the Cloud formed will be?

A. Private Cloud

B. Public Cloud

C. Real Cloud

D. Hybrid Cloud

Question 15

What are the advantages of having infrastructure hosted on the AWS Cloud? Choose two answers:

A. Having the pay as you go, model,

B. Having complete control over the physical infrastructure

C. zero Upfront costs

D. No need to worry about security

Question 16

When instantiating compute resources, what are two techniques for using automated, repeatable processes that are fast and avoid human error? (Select TWO.)

1. Performance monitoring

2. Fault tolerance

3. Snapshotting

4. Infrastructure as code

5. Bootstrapping

Question 17

What strategy can assist with allocating metadata to AWS resources for cost tracking and visibility?

1. Access Control

2. Categorizing

3. Labeling

4. Tagging

Question 18

What is the scope of a VPC within a region?

1. Spans all Availability Zones within the region

2. Spans all Availability Zones globally

3. At least two subnets per region

4. At least 2 data centers per region

Question 19

Which AWS service is primarily used for software version control?

1. AWS CodeDeploy

2. AWS Cloud9

3. AWS CodeStar

4. AWS CodeCommit

Question 20

What benefits does Amazon EC2 provide over using non-cloud servers? (Select TWO.)

1. Complete control of the hypervisor layer

2. Fault tolerance

3. High-availability with an SLA of 99.999%

4. Inexpensive

5. Elastic web-scale computing

Question 21

Which service allows you to expand and shrink your application in response to demand automatically?

1. Amazon EC2 Auto Scaling

2. Amazon DynamoDB

3. AWS ElastiCache

4. Amazon Elastic Load Balancing

Question 22

Which architectural best practice aims to reduce the interdependencies between services?

1. Automation

2. Removing Single Points of Failure

3. Loose Coupling

4. Services, Not Servers

Question 23

An architect wants to find a tool for consistently deploying the same resources through a templated configuration. Which AWS service can be used?

1. AWS CloudFormation

2. AWS Elastic Beanstalk

3. AWS CodeBuild

4. AWS CodeDeploy

Question 24

A company has an application with users in both Australia and Germany. All the company infrastructure is currently provisioned in the Europe (Frankfurt) Region, and Australian users are experiencing high latency.

What should the company do to reduce latency?

1. Launch additional Amazon EC2 instances in Frankfurt to handle the demand

2. Use AWS Transit Gateway to route users from Australia to the application quickly

3. Implement AWS Direct Connect for users in Australia

4. Provision resources in the Asia Pacific (Sydney) Region in Australia

Question 25

Which of the following is a principle of good AWS Cloud architecture design?

1. Implement loose coupling

2. Implement vertical scaling

3. Implement single points of failure

4. Implement monolithic design

CHAPTER 2:

Security

Security is regarded as the highest priority service of AWS. As a user of AWS services, you will be gaining profit from a data center and a network architecture, which has been built to meet all the requirements of the highest organizations, which are security-sensitive. While using the cloud, securing it from all possible sides is of utter importance. Cloud security is somewhat like the security of your on-premises data center. It is of much more critical than the cost of the hardware and maintenance facilities. You are not required to manage the storage devices or physical servers in the cloud. Instead of doing it yourself, you use security tools based on software to protect and monitor the overall flow of information that goes in and out of the cloud resources. It can be done while maintaining a super-secure environment without paying for those services that you do not use at all. It means that you can enjoy premium security and that too at a lesser cost when compared to the protection of your on-premises data center environment. While using AWS's services, you need to inherit all the practices regarding AWS policies, operational processes, and architecture, which have been built for satisfying the ultimate requirements of those customers who are the most security-sensitive. You can enjoy the agility along with flexibility with security services from AWS for your data centers. AWS Cloud comes with a shared responsibility model. While AWS manages the cloud's security, you are the one who is entirely responsible for the security in the cloud. In simple words, you can retain the security control which you choose for protecting your content, applications, platform, networks, and systems in the same way that you would have done for an on-premises data center. You will also receive the required guidance and competence via online personnel, resources, and partners. AWS provides users with various advisories for current issues. You can also enjoy working along with AWS whenever you come across any security issue. To meet up with your cloud security objectives, you also get access to various features and tools. AWS provides the users with tools and features specific to security across network configuration, access control, management, and encryption of data. The AWS environments are audited at regular intervals with certifications from various accreditation bodies across verticals and geographies. You can take full advantage of the automated tools in the AWS environment for access reporting and asset inventory.

Benefits of AWS Security

·   AWS security comes with various benefits that can make your cloud working much more convenient and secure. The infrastructure of AWS puts in place robust safeguards for protecting the privacy of the users. All of your data is stored in super-secure data centers of AWS.

- You can meet compliance requirements with AWS security. AWS is known for managing various programs of compliance within its infrastructure. In simple words, the segments of your required submission have been completed already.

- You can save lots of money with AWS security services. You can cut down your costs with the help of AWS data centers. You can maintain the highest security standards without any need to manage your facility.

- You can scale quickly and conveniently with AWS security services. The security services also scale with the usage of your AWS Cloud. Whatever your business's size, the infrastructure of AWS has been designed to keep all your data safe.

The Shared Responsibility Model

Responsibility on the part of AWS: Security of the Cloud

AWS is solely responsible for the overall protection of its infrastructure that runs all the services offered in the AWS cloud. The infrastructure consists of software, hardware, networking along with all the facilities that run the benefits of AWS cloud. Responsibility on the part of the customer: Security in the Cloud

The obligation on the customer's interest is determined by the services of the AWS cloud selected by the customer. It ultimately determines the overall amount of configuration work that the customer needs to perform as a part of the security responsibilities. For instance, any service of AWS such as Amazon EC2 or Elastic Compute Cloud is being categorized as IaaS or Infrastructure as a Service and requires performance on the part of the customer regarding all the necessary management tasks and configuration of security. Customers who deploy EC2 instance from Amazon are liable for the complete management of the guest O.S. or operating system that also includes the security and update patches, configuration of the firewall provided by AWS, which is known as a security group, and any application utilities or software which is being installed by the customer on the EC2 instances.

For AWS's abstracted services such as DynamoDB or Amazon S3, the infrastructure layer is operated by AWS and the platforms. The customers can easily access the endpoints to retrieve and store the data. The customers are solely responsible for managing their data, including the options of encryption, classification of the assets, and Use of IAM tools for application of the required permissions.

This AWS and customer shared responsibility model also extends itself to the I.T. controls. Like AWS and its customers share the responsibility of the I.T. environment's operations, the operation, management, and verification of the I.T. controls are also shared between the two. AWS can help the customers by relieving the customers' burden to operate the controls by managing all the required rules associated with the infrastructure, which is deployed in the environment of AWS that might have been driven by the AWS customers.

Monitoring And Logging Features

AWS security provides you with various features and tools to have a complete visualization of what is happening in AWS's environment. It also includes:

• Options for log aggregation, compliance reporting, and streamlining the investigations.

• Usage of AWS CloudTrail for having deep visibility into the API calls that also include who, when, what, and where all the needs were made.

• Alert notifications with the help of Amazon CloudWatch whenever thresholds exceed or any specific event occurs.

Identify And Access Management.

AWS security services offer you all the capabilities for defining, managing, and enforcing user access policies across all AWS services. It also includes:

• AWS IAM or Identity and Access Management for determining the respective user account with proper permissions across AWS's resources.

•AWS Directory Service allows you to federate and integrate with the various corporate directories to improve end-user experience and reduce the overhead of administration.

• AWS Multi-Factor Authentication for all the privileged accounts and options for the authenticators based on hardware.

REVIEW QUESTIONS

Question 1:

Under the AWS shared responsibility model, what are the customer's responsibilities? (Select TWO.)

1. Physical network devices, including firewalls

2. Physical and environmental security

3. Security of data in transit

4. Data integrity authentication

5. Storage device decommissioning

Question 2:

According to the AWS shared responsibility model, what are the controls that customers fully inherit from AWS? (Choose two)

A. Communications controls.

B. Environmental controls.

C. Patch Management.

D. Resource Configuration Management.

E. Physical controls.

Question 3:

Which feature can you use to grant read/write access to an Amazon S3 bucket?

1. IAM Role
2. IAM User
3. IAM Policy
4. IAM Group

Question 4:

Which aspects of security on AWS are customer responsibilities? (Select TWO.)

1. Setting up account password policies
2. Patching of storage systems
3. Server-side encryption
4. Availability of AWS regions
5. Physical access controls

Question 5:

Which AWS service is used to enable multi-factor authentication?

1. Amazon STS
2. AWS KMS
3. AWS IAM
4. Amazon EC2

Question 6:

Under the AWS shared responsibility model, what is the customer responsible for? (Select TWO.)

1. Physical security of the data center

2. Patch management of infrastructure

3. Encryption of customer data

4. Configuration of security groups

5. Replacement and disposal of disk drives

Question 7:

Which services are involved with security? (Select TWO.)

1. AWS DMS

2. AWS KMS

3. AWS CloudHSM

4. AWS SMS

5. Amazon ELB

Question 8:

Which of the following should be used to improve the security of access to the AWS Management Console? (Select TWO.)

1. Security group rules

2. AWS Multi-Factor Authentication (AWS MFA)

3. Strong password policies

4. AWS Secrets Manager

5. AWS Certificate Manager

Question 9:

How can an organization assess application for vulnerabilities and deviations from best practice?

1. Use AWS WAF

2. Use AWS Shield

3. Use AWS Inspector

4. Use AWS Artifact

Question 10:

Which AWS service gives you centralized control over the encryption keys used to protect your data?

1. AWS STS

2. Amazon EBS

3. AWS KMS

4. AWS DMS

Question 11:

Which AWS service protects against common exploits that could compromise application availability, compromise security or consume excessive resources?

1. Security Group

2. Network ACL

3. AWS Shield

4. AWS WAF

Question 12:

Which IAM entity can be used for assigning permissions to multiple users?

1. IAM Group

2. IAM User

3. IAM Role

4. IAM password policy

Question 13:

Which IAM entity can be used for assigning permissions to AWS services?

1. Security Token Service (STS)

2. IAM Policy

3. IAM Role

4. IAM Access Key ID and Secret Access Key

Question 14:

Which IAM entity is associated with an access key I.D. and secret access key?

1. IAM Group

2. IAM User

3. IAM Role

4. IAM Policy

Question 15:

How can an organization track resource inventory and configuration history for security and regulatory compliance?

1. Run a report with AWS Artifact

2. Create an Amazon CloudTrail trail

3. Configure AWS Config with the resource types

4. Implement Amazon GuardDuty

Question 16:

Which AWS service provides on-demand downloads of AWS security and compliance reports?

1. AWS Directory Service

2.   AWS Artifact

3.   Amazon Inspector

4.   AWS Trusted Advisor

Question 17

You are going to create snapshots from EBS volumes in another geographical location using the console. Where would you make the snapshots?

A. In another Availability Zone

B. In another data center

C. In another Edge location

D. In another Region

Question 18

What does S3 stand for?

A. Simple Storage Service

B. Simplified Storage Service

C. Simple Store Service

D. Service for Simple Storage

Question 19

Which statement is true regarding the AWS shared responsibility model?

A. The security of the IaaS services is the responsibility of AWS.

B. The security of managed services is the responsibility of the customer.

C. Duties vary depending on the services used.

D. Patching the guest O.S. is the responsibility of AWS for all services.

Question 20

Miller is working with a large data set, and he needs to import it into a relational database service. What AWS service will meet his needs?

A. RDS

B. DynamoDB

C. ElastiCache

D. Neptune

Question 21

What services/features are required to maintain a highly available and fault-tolerant architecture in AWS? (Choose two)

A. Elastic Load Balancer

B. CloudFormation

C. AWS NACL

D. Amazon EC2 Auto Scaling

Question 22

Which of the following aspects of security are managed by AWS? (Choose two)

A. Securing global physical infrastructure

B. Hardware patching

C. VPC security

D. Encryption of EBS volumes

E. Access permissions

Question 23

Which of the following AWS Support Plans gives you 24/7 access to Cloud Support Engineers via email & phone? (Choose two)

A. Premium

B. Developer

C. Business

D. Enterprise

E. Standard

CHAPTER 3:

Technology

AWS Organization and Accounts

Amazon Virtual Private Cloud (VPC)

After a region and AZ have been established, the customer will need a VPC. The VPC is where the customer will launch their AWS resources. It is their logically isolated portion of the cloud that gets assigned for their Use.

Internet Gateway

Next, the internet gateway will be enabled, which grants the customer access to the Internet and sets up the routing tables and network ACL (NACL). A subnet partitions a logical I.P. network into smaller portions or segments, like a housing development built on one property. Instead of one large house on 54 Main Street, there are now ten houses, and their addresses become a subdivision of the primary address.

Security Groups

A security group on AWS is a type of firewall positioned at the instance level of the cloud.

AWS Core Services

AWS comes with a host of core and integrated services to ensure customers get the services they need. These services can be broken into the following:

Database Services

There are several AWS database services, and some of the most widely used ones are:

AWS Relational Database Service (RDS)

RDS is the most commonly used of the database services on AWS because it supports multiple database engines. These database engines include:

- MySQL

- Maria DB

- Oracle

- Aurora

- Microsoft SQL

- Postgres

DymamoDB

It is a database that is based on Cassandra. It is a NoSQL key/value database. It will guarantee many reads or write per second.

ElastiCache

ElastiCache database is a caching source that is compatible with databases such as open-source Memcached and Redis.

Redshift

Redshift is a columnar store database that can run a warehouse-type application that requires petabytes of information. For all those that do not know, one petabyte (P.B.) is 1000 TB.

CloudFormation

It works for infrastructure as code and creates a template using either YAML or JSON file.

Elastic Beanstalk

It is a simple service used for scaling as well as deploying web applications. Elastic Beanstalk is compatible with applications created in .NET, PHP, Node.js, Python, Ruby, Docker, Java, and Go. It is a simple application for uploading code that needs little to no tweaking to work.

AWS Computing

AWS computing core services include the following:

Amazon Elastic Cloud Compute (EC2)

Amazon EC2 is a web service with the following features:

- Provides complete control

- Allows the configuration of capacity

- Provides resizable compute capacity

Everything on AWS runs on EC2 instances. It is an Elastic Compute cloud that allows for the operating system's full configuration, network, memory, and CPU in the cloud environment.

Elastic Container Service (ECS)

This service is highly scalable and provides Docker as a service. It offers high-performance orchestration of containers that supports Docker containers. The customer will have to pay for the EC2 to run this service.

Elastic Beanstalk

Elastic Beanstalk is the service that operates the various AWS services. These services include Simple Notification Services (SNS), EC2 Amazon S3, CloudWatch, Elastic Load Balancers, auto-scaling, and CloudWatch.

Lambda

Lambda is a service that you only pay for when it is in Use. It is a serverless service used to deploy or run code on without having to manage, invest in, or configure servers.

AWS Storage Services

Amazon Elastic Block Store (EBS)

Amazon EBS is used with Amazon EC2 instances to provide block-level storage volumes. EBS volumes exist independently from an example as they are off-instance storage volumes.

They are the virtual disk of the AWS cloud for which there are three types of EBS volumes:

- General Purpose (SSD)
- Magnetic
- Provisional IOPS (SSD)

Amazon Simple Storage Service (S3)

Amazon S3 is an internet or cloud storage space, much like DropBox or GoogleDrive. Only S3 can be used to store any size of data that can be accessed from anywhere over the web.

Amazon S3 features include:

- Object storage
- Can store any amount of data
- S3 is durable
- S3 is scalable
- Uses query in place

- S3 has flexible data management.

- Has flexible data transfer capabilities

- S3 is compatible and supported by AWS services as well as AWS partners, and various vendors.

Elastic File Storage (EFS)

This storage solution can be mounted to two or more EC2 instances at the same time.

Storage Gateway

Storage Gateway bridges the gap for Use with hybrid cloud solutions using local caching.

AWS Logging Services

AWS has a few services that help customers with system audit trails keep a close watch on changes to the AWS system and when those changes were made and by whom.

CloudTrail

CloudTrail audits and logs all calls that were made to APIs from AWS services. This service helps to determine pieces of information such as:

- AWS EC2 instance usage

- Who launched specific applications and when

- Who created a bucket

CloudTrail helps the customer to:

- Determine any misconfiguration that may have been made by a developer or administrator

- Create automated responses

- Help detect and deal with any malicious actors within the system

CloudWatch

CloudWatch comprises a host of different services used for logging information such as performance, various system metrics, and events. It is used to speed up delivery for customers of their content across the globe. Some of these services include:

- CloudWatch Alarms

  o Set threshold alarms, failure alarms, various alerts, etc.

  o Set notifications for various metrics

- CloudWatch Dashboard

  o A metrics-based dashboard that can be customized to visualize various logs, metrics, etc.

- CloudWatch Events

  o Service that will trigger an alarm for set thresholds

REVIEW QUESTIONS

Question 1

Under the AWS shared responsibility model, what are the customer's responsibilities? (Select TWO)

1: Physical and environmental security

2: Physical network devices including firewalls

3: Storage device decommissioning

4: Security of data in transit

5: Data integrity authentication

Question 2

A company plans to deploy a global commercial application on Amazon EC2 instances. The deployment solution is designed with the highest redundancy and fault tolerance.

Based on this situation, how should the EC2 instances be deployed?

1: In a single Availability Zone in one AWS Region

2: In a single Availability Zone in two AWS Regions

3: Across multiple Availability Zones in one AWS Region

4: In various Availability Zones in two AWS Regions

Question 3

Which benefit of the AWS Cloud eliminates the need for users to try estimating future infrastructure usage?

1: Easy global deployments

2: Security of the AWS Cloud

3: Elasticity of the AWS Cloud

4: Economies of scale

Question 4

Which AWS services can be used to connect the AWS Cloud and on-premises resources? (Select TWO)

1: AWS Managed VPN

2: Amazon Connect

3: Amazon CloudHSM

4: AWS Direct Connect

5: AWS Managed Services

Question 5

Where are Amazon EBS snapshots stored?

1: On an Amazon EBS instance store

2: On an Amazon EFS filesystem

3: Within the EBS block store

4: On Amazon S3

Question 6

A company has an application with users in both Australia and Germany. All the company infrastructure is currently provisioned in the Europe (Frankfurt) Region, and Australian users are experiencing high latency.

What should the company do to reduce latency?

1: Implement AWS Direct Connect for users in Australia

2: Provision resources in the Asia Pacific (Sydney) Region in Australia

3: Use AWS Transit Gateway to route users from Australia to the application quickly

4: Launch additional Amazon EC2 instances in Frankfurt to handle the demand

Question 7

Which AWS Support plan provides access to architectural and operational reviews, as well as 24/7 access to Cloud Support Engineers through email, online chat, and phone?

1: Basic

2: Business

3: Developer

4: Enterprise

Question 8

Which benefits can a company immediately realize using the AWS Cloud? (Select TWO)

1: Variable expenses are replaced with capital expenses

2: Capital expenses are replaced with variable expenses

3: User control of physical infrastructure

4: Increased agility

5: No responsibility for security

Question 9

Which service will enable you to run code as functions without needing to provision or manage servers?

1: Amazon EC2

2: AWS CodeDeploy

3: AWS Lambda

4: Amazon EKS

Question 10

An application that is deployed across multiple Availability Zones could be described as:

1: Being highly available

2: Having a global reach

3: Being secure

4: Having elasticity

Question 11

Which AWS tools can be used for automation? (Select TWO)

1: AWS Elastic Beanstalk

2: Elastic Load Balancing

3: AWS CloudFormation

4: Amazon Elastic File System (EFS)

5: AWS Lambda

Question 12

A user has an AWS account with a Business-level AWS Support plan and needs assistance with handling a production service disruption. Which action should the user take?

1: Contact the dedicated Technical Account Manager

2: Contact the dedicated AWS Concierge Support team

3: Open a business-critical system down support case

4: Open a production system down support case

Question 13

How does "elasticity" benefit an application design?

1: By reducing interdependencies between application components

2: By automatically scaling resources based on demand

3: By selecting the correct storage tier for your workload

4: By reserving capacity to reduce cost

Question 14

Which AWS storage technology can be considered a "virtual hard disk in the cloud"?

1: Amazon Elastic File Storage (EFS) filesystem

2: Amazon Elastic Block Storage (EBS) volume

3: Amazon S3 object

4: Amazon Glacier archive

Question 15

What is the scope of a VPC within a region?

1: Spans all Availability Zones within the region

2: Spans all Availability Zones globally

3: At least two subnets per region

4: At least 2 data centers per region

Question 16

A company needs protection from distributed denial of service (DDoS) attacks on its website and assistance from AWS experts during such events. Which AWS managed service will meet these requirements?

1: AWS Shield Advanced

2: AWS Firewall Manager

3: AWS Web Application Firewall

4: Amazon GuardDuty

Question 17

Which AWS security service provides a firewall at the subnet level within a VPC?

1: Security Group

2: IAM Policy

3: Bucket Policy

4: Network Access Control List

Question 18

Which AWS Cloud design principles can help increase reliability? (Select TWO)

1: Using monolithic architecture

2: Measuring overall efficiency

3: Testing recovery procedures

4: Adopting a consumption model

5: Automatically recovering from failure

Question 19

Which items can be configured from within the VPC management console? (Select TWO)

1: Subnets

2: Regions

3: Load Balancing

4: Auto Scaling

5: Security Groups

Question 20

Which of the following are accurate descriptions of AWS IAM users and groups? (Select TWO)

1: Groups can be nested and can contain other groups

2: A user can be a member of multiple groups

3: Groups can have users only and cannot be nested

4: A user can only be a member of a single group at one a time

5: All new users are automatically added to a default group

Question 21

What considerations are there when choosing which region to use? (Select TWO)

1: Data sovereignty

2: Available storage capacity

3: Latency

4: Pricing in local currency

5: Available compute capacity

Question 22

What technology enables calculate the ability to adjust as loads change?

1: Load balancing

2: Automatic failover

3: Round robin

4: Auto Scaling

Question 23

Based on the shared responsibility model, which of the following security and compliance tasks is AWS responsible for?

1: Granting access to individuals and services

2: Encrypting data in transit

3: Updating Amazon EC2 host firmware

4: Updating operating systems

Question 24

Which AWS technology can be referred to as a "virtual hard disk in the cloud"?

1: Amazon EFS Filesystem

2: Amazon S3 Bucket

3: Amazon EBS volume

4: Amazon ENI

Question 25

Which type of scaling does Amazon EC2 Auto Scaling provide?

1: Vertical

2: Linear

3: Horizontal

4: Incremental

CHAPTER 4:

Billing and Pricing

Reliability Design Principles

AWS advocates several design principles to enhance the reliability of your solution:

1. Testing recovery procedures
2. Automatically recover from failure
3. Scale horizontally to increase aggregate system availability.
4. Stop guessing capacity
5. Manage change in automation

Areas of Reliability

AWS partitions reliability into three areas:

1. Foundations
2. Change Management
3. Failure Management

AWS Reliability Foundations Services

The AWS reliability foundations services include:

1. AWS IAM

2. Amazon VPC

3. AWS Trusted Advisor

4. AWS Shield

The AWS IAM, VPC, and Shield are covered elsewhere in this manuscript. Please refer to the table of contents.

AWS Trusted Advisor

At no charge, every AWS account has access to the AWS Trusted Advisor. Accessed from the AWS Management Console, the AWS Trusted Advisor helps AWS customers improve security and performance. Its prominent focus is on:

- Service Limits

- Security Groups

- Specific Ports Unrestricted

- IAM use

- MFA on the AWS Root Account

- Find under-utilized resources

The AWS Trusted Advisor provides customers with easy access to a variety of important performance and security recommendations. As reported by AWS, the most popular proposals involve:

- Cost optimization
- Security
- Fault tolerance
- Performance improvement; and
- Service checks
- The AWS Trusted Advisor is also a source of best practices that cover:
- Service limits;
- Security group rules that allow unrestricted access to specific ports ;
- IAM use;
- MFA on the root account;
- S3 bucket permissions;
- EBS public snapshots, and
- RDS available snapshots.

For AWS clients who have purchased the Business or Enterprise Support plans, there are additional checks and guidance available.

AWS Reliability Change Management Services

The AWS reliability change management services include:

- AWS CloudTrail
- AWS Config
- Amazon CloudWatch – this is the AWS service that is key to ensuring reliability.
- Auto Scaling

The above services are covered elsewhere in this manuscript. Please refer to the table of contents.

AWS Reliability Failure Management Services

The AWS reliability failure management services include:

- AWS CloudFormation
- Amazon S3
- Amazon Glacier
- AWS KMS

The above services are covered elsewhere in this manuscript. Please refer to the table of contents.

Reliability Design Patterns

In the AWS cloud, there are four common reliability design patterns:

1. Backup and Restore

2. Pilot Light Architecture

3. Fully Working Low-Capacity Standby Architecture

4. Multi-site Active-Active Architecture

Their preparation and disaster recovery phases will be explained for each design pattern. Then their RTO and RPO will be described.

Backup and Restore

The best that can be said of reliability based on backup and restore best practices is that the approach minimizes costs (i.e., you pay for storage of the backup images) and a simple solution that is easy to get started with.

Preparation Phase: Level 0 backup images of each system component have to be taken, and incremental backup photos are taken subsequently. These backup image files are stored in S3. To be able to restore the system' know-how' covering these matters are mandatory and must also be documented: which AMI to use/build, restoring from a backup image, configuring the deployment, smoothly switching over to the recovered components.

Disaster Recovery Phase: restore failed component(s) from their backup images, launch required infrastructure, switching over to the recovered/established parts.

RTO: this takes as long as it takes to restore from backup and then launch and switch over.

RPO: since the last time the backup image was made.

Pilot Light Architecture

A typical Pilot Light Architect has an on-premise system (the primary), which the DNS service (e.g., Amazon Route 53 points to). And in the AWS cloud, you have a secondary system that includes a replicate database that is a mirror image of the on-premise database. The other application components are also present in the cloud, but they are all minimally provisioned resources.

Preparation Phase: though the other application components are provisioned in the cloud, they are not running (other than the data replication processes). Of course, backups are being taken regularly, and recovery procedures must be fully documented and well known.

Disaster Recovery Phase: when the primary fails, the cloud components are automatically up-scaled and launched. The DNS service is then changed to point to the backup system now running in the AWS cloud.

RTO: the time it takes to detect the primary system failure and the automated provisioning of the AWS cloud's secondary system.

RPO: this depends on the frequency of data replication between the primary and the secondary.

Fully Working Low-Capacity Standby Architecture

In the fully working low-capacity standby architecture, there are two running systems, the fully provisioned primary and a low-capacity secondary, to which the DNS server is distributing requests. In this example, the low-capacity secondary is running in the AWS cloud.

Preparation Phase: the low-capacity secondary must be designed and built to auto-scale horizontally.

Disaster Recovery Phase: immediately begin to failover to the secondary, the low-capacity secondary is auto-scaled to match the capacity of the now-failed primary system, and the DNS server is changed to point only to the AWS cloud secondary system

RTO: as long as it takes the secondary to scale-up to primary capacity.

RPO: directly dependent on the type of data replication system being used.

Reliability Best Practices

AWS recommends the following reliability best practices:

1. Start simple and work towards more complex automation;
2. Be sure to take full backups of the AWS solutions;
3. Incrementally improve the RTO and RPO on an ongoing basis;
4. Exercise and practice disaster recovery procedures.

REVIEW QUESTIONS

Question 1

A company wants to monitor all events in their AWS account; in such a case, which of the following can help them out?

A. AWS S3

B. AWS CloudTrail

C. AWS TCO

D. AWS Trusted advisor

Question 2

Choose the options which correctly mention the responsibility of AWS according to the Shared Security Model? Choose three answers :

A. Securing edge locations

B. Managing Console

C. Monitoring physical device security

D. Implementing service organization Control (SOC) standards

Question 3

For non-stop Monitoring, logging, and auditing of physical access controls, which tool can be used?

A. Physical Security

B. User keyword

C. Local Guidance

D. Tertiary Security

Question 4

When public and private cloud services are mixed, the cloud formed will be?

A. Private Cloud

B. Public Cloud

C. Real Cloud

D. Hybrid Cloud

Question 5

A company wants to use an application where there is a significant amount of traffic. Which services can help them?

A. Single-purpose IOPS

B. General Purpose IOPS

C. Provisioned IOPS

D. Multipurpose IOPS

Question6

Can you suggest any other name for attributes?

A.   Series

B.   Indexes

C.   Fields

D.   Keys

Question 7

Select one of the vital features on Navigation Bar?

A. AWS S3

B. AWS Monitor Control

C. AWS Menu bar

D. AWS Region

Question 8

Direct Attached Storage is a kind of _____ Storage.

A. Amazon Elastic Block Storage

B. Read drive

C. Hard Disk Storage

D. Internal Storage

Question 9

A category recommendation that is not given by the AWS Trusted Advisor?

A. Groups

B. Low availability

C. Cost Optimization

D. Discipline

E. High Availability

Question 10

Let's suppose you have a Web application hosted in an EC2 Instance that needs to send notifications based on events. What service can you get help from?

A. AWS MFA

B. AWS SNS

C. AWS EC2

D. AWS EBS

Question 11

For transfer of a website to one type of cloud while its brochure is on another, which cloud can be used?

A. Real Cloud

B. Private Cloud

C. Dynamic Cloud

D. Hybrid Cloud

Question 12

Suppose you want to access the provided service in AWS, what do you prefer?

A. AWS Security Groups

B. AWS Hardware Development Kits

C. AWS Software Development Kits

D. AWS Enquiry API?s

Question 13

Your organization wants to use high-frequency processors, which instance type will you prefer?

A. Dedicated

B. M2

C. C3

D. On spot

Question 14

At the time of the disaster, what actions will you perform to safeguard your company?

A. Close your datacenter

B. Backup your mission static data

C. Scalable computing capacity routers

D. Launch the replacement compute capacity

Question 15

Choose any of the following two security requirements that are managed by AWS customers?

A. Physical security

B. Tertiary security

C. Password Policies

D. User permissions

E. Hardware patching

Question 16

When calculating Total Cost of Ownership (TCO) for the AWS Cloud, which factor must be considered?

A. The ability to choose the highest cost vendor

B. The number of users migrated out of AWS

C. The number of servers migrated to AWS

D. The number of users migrated to AWS

Question 17

A company wants access to all the checks in the Trusted Advisor Service, how can they do it? Choose two options.

A. Business

B. Enterprise

C. Account

D. Department

Question 18

XYZ company wants to use network services that would implement its code from Amazon EC2 instances on the virtual servers. What should the company use?

A. AWS console

B. Amazon E.C. dashboard

C. manual Scaling Service

D. AWS Lambda

Question 19

Choose the most appropriate option to use the DNS Web service?

A.   Amazon Route 53 Hosted Zones

B.   Manual Scaling Groups

C.   Hybrid cloud

D.   Private cloud

Question 20

Elastic Load Balancer has a higher fault-tolerance level. How?

A. Dividing instances into several Availability Zones

B. Launch the replacement compute capacity

C. Multiplying examples into one availability Zones

D. Destroying subnets

Question 21

Choose the option that is a scalable and economic amalgamation of your office I.T. and AWS storage infrastructure?

A. AWS MFA

B. AWS EBS Volume

C. Amazon CLI

D. AWS Storage Gateway

Question 22

What was the first service offered by Amazon to transfer data?

A. Disk

B. Snowball

C. AWS CLI

D. AWS POLICIES

Question 23

To examine the customer's AWS environment, identify security gaps, and fill them, which tool in AWS can be used?

A. Trusted Guide

B. Trusted Advisor

C. Trusted Counselor

D. Trusted Controller

Question 24

A part of the Enterprise support plan, which is the primary point of contact for the ongoing support needs?

A. TSM

B. SQL

C. SBS

D. TAM

Question 25

Which can be a fair use case for storing content in AWS RRS?

A. Storing large video files.

B. Keeping thumbnails & transcoded media

C. Storing a video file which is not producible

D. Storing frequently used log files.

CHAPTER 5:

AWS Services

The AWS administration that is fundamental to Reliability is Amazon CloudWatch, which screens runtime measurements. The associated administrations and highlights bolster the three regions in dependability:

· Foundations: AWS IAM empowers you to control access to AWS administrations, furthermore, assets safely. AWS Trusted Consultant gives perceivability into administration limits. AWS Shield is an overseen Distributed Forswearing of Service (DDoS) insurance administration that shields web applications are running on AWS.

· AWS Config gives a point by point stock of your AWS assets and setup, and persistently records design changes. Amazon AutoScaling is a help that will provide a computerized request to the executives for a conveyed outstanding task at hand. Amazon CloudWatch gives the capacity to alert on measurements, including custom measurements. Amazon CloudWatch likewise has logging include that it can utilize to total log records from your assets.

· Failure Management: AWS CloudFormation gives formats to the production of AWS assets and arrangements them in an organized and unsurprising manner. Amazon S3 offers profoundly sturdy assistance to keep reinforcements. Amazon Glacier gives exceptionally sturdy documents. AWS KMS provides a robust essential administration framework that incorporates numerous AWS administrations.

Execution Efficiency

The Performance Efficiency column incorporates the capacity to utilize processing assets productively to meet framework prerequisites and keep up that effectiveness as request changes and advances develop. You can discover prescriptive direction on Execution in the Execution Efficiency Pillar whitepaper.

The Standard for Execution:

There are five plan standards for execution proficiency in the cloud:

Democratize Cutting Edge Innovations:

Technologies that are hard to actualize can get simpler to devour by driving that information and multifaceted nature into the cloud seller's space. As opposed to having your I.T. group figure out how to have, what's more, run another innovation, they can permanently expend it as a help. For instance, NoSQL databases, media transcoding, and A.I. are generally advances that require the ability that isn't uniformly scattered over the specialized network. In the cloud, these innovations become administrations that your group can devour while concentrating on item improvement instead of asset provisioning.

Go worldwide in minutes:

Easily convey your framework in various regions around the world with only a couple of snaps. It permits you to give lower idleness and a superior experience for your clients at negligible expense.

Use serverless structures:

In the cloud, serverless designs evacuate the need to run and keep up servers to do conventional figure exercises. For model, stockpiling administrations can go about as static sites, expelling the requirement for web servers, and occasionally have your code for you. It does not just evacuate the operational weight of dealing with these servers. Yet, it can also bring down value-based costs because these oversaw administrations work at a cloud-scale. Test all the more regularly: With virtual and automatable assets, you can rapidly do comparative testing utilizing various kinds of cases, stockpiling, or setups.

Mechanical compassion:

Use the innovative approach that adjusts best to what you are attempting to achieve. For instance, consider information that gets to designs while choosing a database or capacity draws near.

Definition of execution proficiency in the cloud:

There are best practice zones for execution proficiency in the cloud:

· Selection

· Monitoring

· Trade-offs

Adopt an information-driven strategy in choosing elite engineering. Assemble information on all parts of the engineering, from the significant level structure to the determination, what's the more, design of asset types. By evaluating your decisions on a patterned premise, you will guarantee that you are exploiting the consistently advancing AWS Cloud. Checking will ensure that you know about any Cost Optimization.

Cost Optimization:

The Cost Optimization column incorporates the capacity to run frameworks to convey business esteem at the most reduced value point. The cost streamlining column gives a diagram of plan standards, best practices also, questions. You can discover prescriptive direction on usage in the Cost improvement Pillar whitepaper.

Plan Principles of Cost Improvement in the Cloud:

There are five structure standards for cost improvement in the cloud:

· Adopt a utilization model: Pay just for the figuring assets that you require and increment or diminishing use contingent upon business necessities, not by utilizing elaborate determining. For instance, improvement and test situations are commonly just used for eight hours per day during the workweek. You can stop these assets when they not used for a potential cost reserve funds of 75%

· Measure by and significant effectiveness: Measure the business yield of the remaining task at hand and the costs related to conveying it. Utilize this Measure to know the increases you make from expanding return and diminishing expenses.

· Stop burning through cash on server farm activities: AWS does the challenging work of racking, stacking, and controlling servers to concentrate on your clients and association extends as opposed to on I.T. foundation.

· Analyze and private consumption: The cloud makes it simpler to precisely distinguish the utilization and cost of frameworks, which at that point permits straightforward attribution of I.T. costs to singular remaining burden proprietors. These assist measures with returning on venture (ROI) and offer outstanding tasks at hand proprietors to upgrade their assets and diminish costs.

· Use oversaw and application-level administrations to decrease the cost of possession: In the cloud, managed and application-level administrations expel the operational weight of keeping up servers for errands, for example, sending an email or overseeing databases. As overseen administrations work at a cloud-scale, they can offer a lower cost for each exchange or, on the other hand, administration.

There are four best practice zones for cost improvement in the cloud:

· Consumption Awareness

· Cost-Effective Resources

· Matching market interest

· Optimizing Over Time

Similarly, as with different columns, there are trade-offs to consider. For instance, do you need to organize for speed to advertise or for cost? Now and again, it's ideal for organizing for speed—going to announce rapidly, transporting new highlights, or necessarily complying with a time constraint — as opposed to putting resources into direct cost streamlining. Plan choices are now and again guided by flurry rather than observational information, as the enticement consistently exists to overcompensate "in the event of some unforeseen issue" as opposed to investing energy benchmarking for the most cost-ideal remaining burden after some time. It frequently prompts over-provisioned what's more, under-upgraded arrangements, which stay static for a mind-blowing duration cycle. The associated segments give procedures and critical direction to the underlying and continuous cost enhancement of your method.

Consumption Awareness

The expanded adaptability and skill that the cloud empowers energizes advancement and quick-paced advancement and arrangement. It dispenses with the manual procedures and time-related with provisioning on-premises framework, including recognizing equipment particulars, arranging value citations, overseeing buy orders, planning shipments, and afterward conveying the assets. Be that as it may, the convenience what's more, for all intents and purposes boundless on-request limit, requires another perspective about consumptions.

Numerous organizations are made out of different frameworks run by other groups. The capacity to credit asset expenses to the individual association or item proprietors drives active utilization conduct and diminishes squander. Exact cost attribution permits you to know which items are productive and allows you to make more educated choices about where to assign spending plan.

In AWS, you can utilize Cost Explorer to follow your spending and increase bits of knowledge into precisely where you spend. Utilizing AWS Budgets, you can send warnings if your Use or, on the other hand, costs are not in line with your figures. You can utilize labeling on assets to apply business and association data to your utilization and value; this gives extra bits of knowledge to advancement from an association point of view.

Upgrading Over Time

As AWS discharges new administrations and highlights, it is a best practice to audit your current

structural choices to guarantee they keep on being the savviest. As your necessities change, be forceful in decommissioning assets, whole administrations, and frameworks that you do not require anymore. Overseen administrations from AWS can altogether enhance the remaining burden, so it is fundamental to know about new oversaw administrations and highlights as they become accessible. For a model, running an Amazon RDS database can be less expensive than running your Amazon EC2. The associated inquiries centeron these contemplations for cost advancement.

CHAPTER 6:

How to Secure Your AWS Resources

If you have created your account, the next step is securing your AWS resources. You need to follow some security best practices to safeguard your help in the cloud. After creating your account with a favorite e-mail and password in AWS's management console, you should always sign in your root account with these same credentials.

Avoid compromising your root account by adopting security best practices.

The root account contains all resources and services in your account. Here are some tips to securing your account:

Creating a Strong Password for your Account in the Cloud

Use a strong password for your account. It involves a combination of numerals, memorable characters, and letters.

It uses a third-party management tool for passwords designed to create and manage strong passwords.

Using a Group E-mail Alias

This feature enables other trusted members of your organization to access the account if you are unavoidably absent from responding to e-mails, notifications, and manage workloads in the cloud. You can also update your details in your account at any time.

Enable or Apply Multi-Factor Authentication Process

The multi-factor authentication process is a security feature providing an extra level of protection to your root account and your username and password.

After signing in to your account with your user name and password, you should include an additional piece of information accessible to you alone.

It is stored in a phone, app, or a reliable MFA hardware system.

Choose the type of multi-factor authentication device to use from the list of supported devices on the platform.

If you are using a hardware system for storing your MFA, ensure the device is kept in a safe place.

If your MFA is a virtual system such as software or phone, consider what happens to your passwords and e-mail addresses if the app is corrupted or missing.

The best method is to activate more than one device at once. You can also use a virtual system with options for password recovery.

Daily Account Access requires you to setup Groups, Users, and Roles.

If more than one person or various groups will be managing the system every day, create user groups and roles using the IAM (Identity and Access Management) resources.

Activating this type of accessibility on the cloud will only grant permission to the IAM user group with specific roles that they are allowed to do in the system. It is also called the least privilege in Amazon Web Services.

Delete or Remove your Account's Access Keys

Using the command line together with Amazon APIs, you can allow programmatic access to your AWS resources. It is recommended that users should not create or use the access keys or passwords associated with their accounts for programmatic access into the cloud.

If you already have access keys, it is advisable to delete or remove them. However, create IAM users and grant such persons the necessary permissions they need to execute their workloads. It will enable you to issue access keys to your groups with the IAM user.

CloudTrail Should be Enabled

Enabling CloudTrail helps you in tracking every activity in your AWS resources. Turn on your cloud platform; this will assist the support center and your solutions engineer in devising possible security issues or configuration problems.

Identity and Accessibility Management in AWS

Now, you can enjoy secure accessibility and manage your AWS services and resources properly using AWS IAM – Identity and Access Management. With this, you can create and manage your user groups. It will enable you to use permissions to allow or deny access to unauthorized persons. This feature is provided at no cost, but charges are incurred by using other AWS resources.

How Identity and Accessibility Management Works

a. Helps you manage the roles and permissions – IAM helps you create roles and manage their permissions in handling operations and services that could be performed by an entity or AWS service assuming the position. It enables you to define persons that can take specific roles in the platform. Another feature here is called service-linked functions that can help you to delegate permissions and roles to cloud resources on your behalf. b. Handles Users and Accessibility – it is easy to create users and assign them personal security credentials such as passwords, access keys, and MFA. You can also demand temporary security credentials to provide users access to cloud resources and services. It is necessary to control permissions and regulate who can access the platform at any time.

c. Controls Federated Users and Permissions – identity federation for existing identities is a great feature for managing groups, users, and delegating roles. Apply other identity management solutions that support SAML 2.0, or you can use federation samples such as API federation or AWS Console SSO.

Best Practices for Identity and Accessibility Management in AWS

The best practices for IAM in AWS include:

· Turning on AWS CloudTrail for auditing.

· Enabling MFA for privileged users.

· Rotating security credentials regularly.

· Restricting exceptional accessibility further with conditions.

· Removing or reducing the Use of the root.

· Using IAM roles for sharing access to the platform.

· Applying IAM roles for Amazon EC2 instances.

· Configuring and maintaining a firm password policy.

· Creating individual users.

· Managing permissions with groups.

· Granting or offering the least privilege to users.

Use Cases for IAM in Amazon Web Services

1. Offers multi-factor authentication for privileged customers – high privileged users can access the cloud resources at no additional costs.

It will provide them with the user name and password credentials. Moreover, users are requested to have a token for hardware MFA or use MFA-enabled mobile device with a valid MFA code.

2. Analyzing access across your AWS environment – with IAM in AWS, you can analyze access across your domain to enable your security administrators and teams to authenticate that your policies can provide the public and other users easy access to your online resources. These policies could be refined to give access to only the right services needed by users.

3. IAM integrates with your corporate directory – this feature grants your workers or users and applications federated access to the AWS service APIs and AWS management console. It is possible with existing identity systems like Microsoft's active directory. Other identity management solution supporting SAML 2.0 or federation samples such as API federation.

4. Provides Smooth access to AWS resources – this feature gives you unrestricted access to AWS service APIs, including specific cloud resources. It enables you to add the time of day that someone can access the platform, including their original I.P. addresses. This case will indicate if the users have SSL or they have authenticated an MFA device.

Authentication Processes

The authentication process of your Identity and Accessibility Management is done using a multi-factor authentication process. It is an easy best practice that adds a layer of protection to your user name and password in the cloud.

It involves a two-step process for verifying your accessibility to the cloud platform.

a. If you sign in to the AWS management console, you will be prompted to enter your user name and password. That is the first factor, which is based on what you know.

b. The second factor is that you will be requested to put in an authentication code for your Amazon Web Service MFA device.

Both of these authentication processes provide a reliable security feature for your AWS resources and account settings. This authentication process could be enabled for your personal IAM users created under your account name. The multi-factor authentication process could be used for controlling accessibility to service APIs in Amazon Web Services. No charges will be made on your AWS account after setting up a supported hardware device or virtual multi-factor authentication device. Cross-account accessibility to the cloud platform can be protected using MFA procedures.

The Roles of User Groups in AWS

User groups could be assigned an existing IAM role in the directory of Amazon Web Services. There should be a reliable relationship with the AWS directory service.

Here are the processes to assign groups of users to existing IAM user groups in AWS.

· Scroll to the navigation pane of Amazon Web Services (AWS) directory service console and click on Directories.

· On the drop-down menu on the Directories page, select your directory I.D.

· Go to the directory details menu and click on the Application management button.

· Scroll to the AWS Management console menu and click on Delegate console access. Select the IAM role name for an existing IAM role, which you want to assign to other users. If you notice that the function has not yet been created, see Creating a New Role.

· Click on the selected or designated role menu page. Go to Manage Users and groups for this role and click the Add button.

· Go to the Add groups or users to the role menu page and click on choose active directory Forest

Select the on-premises forest, a trusted forest, or Amazon Web Services managed Microsoft A.D. forest, referred to as this forest. Either of these forests is designed for accessing the AWS management console.

· Locate and click on Specify which groups or users to add. Choose either Find by Group or Find by User. Enter the name of the group or user in the box provided. Use the list on the menu page to add for possible matches with your desired group.

· Click on Add and finish assigning the groups and users to the role.

Access for users in nested groups in your directory is not supported. Members or users of the parent group have access to the console, while children groups don't have such access.

Conclusion

Amazon continues to roll out new regional places, so you're most likely to have access to a neighboring service location and the abundant AWS ecosystem.

AWS Is the Leading Cloud-Computing Provider. AWS is exceptionally popular. However, its popularity has the impact of making the service much better. Today, Amazon has an enhancing cycle taking place:

- Having more users produces a higher volume of usage, which increases the amount of hardware Amazon purchases, which reduces its costs utilizing economies of scale, which are handed down to users in the type of lower prices.

-Because of the large number of users, companies that use complimentary services (online application integration, for example) decide to initially put their services in AWS, which makes the total service much better, which draws in more users.

-As more people and companies use AWS, more understanding is made available in human capital and other resources (like this book!).

This knowledge makes it easier for new users to start and be productive quickly, making AWS more attractive.

AWS's popularity and acknowledge that its status as the most prominent cloud provider brings considerable advantages to you and that, moreover, those benefits will continue to grow as the service. It's another present that keeps providing.

AWS Enables Innovation.

Everywhere you turn, the word development is a hot subject. Individuals acknowledge that innovation makes life much better and can improve the future for generations to come. All of the incumbent innovation market leaders had no reward for altering the method they did the company.

AWS has changed how technology is provided to clients and, as a result, has enabled a surge of development. The development and low cost related to AWS permit little and big business to rapidly and cheaply introduce brand-new offerings as one development consultant put it:

AWS has decreased the cost of failure. AWS lets you quickly check out a brand-new item to see whether it "gets traction. On the other hand, if the service does not attain adoption, that's no issue-- the ease of shutting down. AWS resources mean that very little is lost if an ingenious perspective offering does not turn out.".meanorecast that a lot more innovation will happen as more individuals and companies become knowledgeable about AWS and its capabilities. AWS will be to the details.

AWS Is Cost Effective.

Much of that expense reduction is because of AWS: its on-demand low prices and simple termination without any charges make it possible to utilize and spend precisely as much computing capacity as you require when you require it.

The expense effectiveness of AWS isn't limited to start-ups, though. Every company can take advantage of access to inexpensive computing that doesn't need a prolonged commitment. It's a sign of the significantbenefits of AWS that much.

When there, the existing supplier community is terrified of what will occur.

Customers begin to demand AWS-like prices and benefit from them.

Amazon is a different company. Unlike many companies that strive for effectiveness to raise their own earnings margins, Amazon passes on the advantages of energy at lower costs. There's no factor to anticipate that this method will change.

It's substantially more expense significant than the conventional mode of acquiring.

By far, the leading cloud computing supplier in the industry, Amazon Web Services, is growing at rates of more than 100 percent. Its record of innovation and rate competitiveness is unrivaled in the market. I forecast that ten years from now, AWS will be the Microsoft or Google of its period. Your organization should become knowledgeable about AWS and determine how to utilize it successfully-- otherwise, it may discover itself the IT equivalent of a buggy whip maker after Henry Ford developed the assembly line.

AWS Is Good for Your Career.

Great careers are constructed on being the best individual in the best location at the right time. Being the best individual is all about you-- your capability for effort, Productive work relationships, and intelligence. These attributes will assist you to succeed no matter which field or function you operate in.

However, remaining in the ideal place at the perfect time has a lot to do with insight about where a brand-new market, made possible by some development, is emerging and planting your flag there. In the 1920s or into the tv service in the 1950s or the Internet in the 1990s, people who moved into the vehicle industry experienced enormous opportunities as a new market searched for expertise to enable terrific companies to be built.

Technology innovation produces powerful abilities gaps in the market and makes those with understanding and experience necessary. Suppose you think that AWS is. The next-generation platform, too, can represent "the best place at the time" for you.

Answers to Review Questions

Cloud Concepts

Question1 Answer(s): 3, 4

Explanation:

Subnets and Security groups can be configured from within the VPC console.

CORRECT: "Subnets" is the right answer.

CORRECT: "Security Groups" is the right answer.

INCORRECT: "Regions" is incorrect. Regions are not configured, resources within regions are configured.

INCORRECT: "Load Balancing" is incorrect. Load balancing is configured from the EC2 console.

INCORRECT: "Auto Scaling" is incorrect. Auto scaling is configured from the EC2 console.

Question 2 Answer: 4

Explanation:

Elasticity means that your infrastructure scales are based on actual usage. When you have higher demand, you use more infrastructure and pay more, and when you have less demand, you need less infrastructure and pay less. The benefits are you don't need to guess about capacity and pay only for what you need.

CORRECT: "Elasticity of the AWS Cloud" is the right answer.

INCORRECT: "Easy global deployments" is incorrect. It is easy to deploy many AWS resources globally. Still, this benefit does not eliminate the need to estimate future usage.

INCORRECT: "Security of the AWS Cloud" is incorrect. The security of the AWS Cloud is important but does not eliminate the need to estimate future usage.

INCORRECT: "Economies of scale" is incorrect. This means you pay less for some resources because of the benefits of AWS's scale. However, this benefit does not eliminate the need to estimate future usage.

Question 3 Answer: 4

Explanation:

Only the Enterprise plan provides a response time of < 15 minutes for the failure of a business-critical system.

Both Business and Enterprise offer < 1-hour response time for the failure of a production system.

CORRECT: "Enterprise" is the right answer.

INCORRECT: "Business" is incorrect as described above.

INCORRECT: "Basic" is incorrect as described above.

INCORRECT: "Developer" is incorrect as described above.

Question 4 Answer(s):3, 5

Explanation:

Shared Controls– Controls which apply to both the infrastructure layer and customer layers, but in completely separate contexts or perspectives

Patch Management– AWS is responsible for patching and fixing flaws within the infrastructure, but customers are responsible for patching their guest OS and applications

Configuration Management– AWS maintains the configuration of itsinfrastructuredevices. Still, a customer is responsible for configuring their own guest operating systems, databases, and applications.

CORRECT: "Patch management" is a right answer.

CORRECT: "Configuration management" is also theright answer.

INCORRECT: "Storage system patching" is incorrect. Storage system patching is an AWS responsibility.

INCORRECT: "Physical and environmental" is incorrect. Physical and Environmental controls is an example of an inherited power (a customer fully inherits from AWS).

INCORRECT: "Service and Communications Protection" is incorrect. Service and Communications Protection is an example of a customer specific control.

Question 5 Answer: 1

Explanation:

Elasticity allows you to deploy your application without worrying about whether it will need more or fewer resources in the future. With elasticity, the infrastructure can scale on-demand, and you only pay for what you use.

CORRECT: "Elasticity" is the right answer.

Question 6 Answer: 2, 4

Explanation:

Amazon S3 uses a universal (global) namespace, which means bucket names must be unique globally. However, you create the buckets in a region, and the data never leaves that region unless explicitly configured to do so through cross-region replication (CRR).

CORRECT: "Bucket names must be unique globally," is the right answer.

CORRECT: "Buckets are region-specific" is also a right answer.

INCORRECT: "Bucket names must be unique regionally" is incorrect as they must be globally unique.

INCORRECT: "Buckets are replicated globally," is incorrect. Objects within a bucket are replicated within a region across multiple AZs (except for the One-Zone IA class).

INCORRECT: "Buckets can contain other buckets" is incorrect. You cannot create nested buckets.

Question 7 Answer: 4, 5

Explanation:

The AWS Global infrastructure is built around Regions and Availability Zones (AZs). A Region is a physical location in the world where AWS has multiple AZs. AZs consist of one or more discrete data centers, each with redundant power, networking, and connectivity, housed in separate facilities

CORRECT: "Regions" is a right answer.

CORRECT: "Availability Zones" is also a right answer.

INCORRECT: "Clusters" is incorrect as this is not part of the AWS global infrastructure.

INCORRECT: "Fault Zones" is incorrect as this is not part of the AWS global infrastructure.

INCORRECT: "IP subnets" is incorrect as this is not part of the AWS global infrastructure.

Question 8 Answer: 2

Explanation:

S3 One Zone-IA is for data that is accessed less frequently, but requires rapid access when needed. Unlike other S3 Storage Classes which store data in a minimum of three Availability Zones (AZs), S3

One Zone-IA stores data in a single AZ and costs 20% less than S3 Standard-IA.

It's a good choice for storing secondary backup copies of on-premises data or easily re-creatable data. You can also use it as cost-effective storage for data that is replicated from another AWS Region using S3 Cross-Region Replication.

CORRECT: "Amazon S3 One Zone-Infrequent Access" is the right answer.

INCORRECT: "Amazon S3 Standard" is incorrect as this is a more resilient storage class and will cost more, so it not optimized for these requirements.

INCORRECT: "Amazon S3 Glacier Deep Archive" is incorrect. This storage class is suited to archival and takes several hours to restore data.

INCORRECT: "Amazon S3 Glacier" is incorrect. This storage class is suited to archival and takes minutes to hours to restore data.

Question 9 Answer: 2

Explanation:

Bootstrapping is the execution of automated actions to services such as EC2 and RDS. This is typically in the form of scripts that run when the instances are launched.

CORRECT: "Bootstrapping" is the right answer.

INCORRECT: "Golden Images" is incorrect. Golden Images are snapshots of pre-configured EBS volumes that can be used to launch new instances. You do this using Amazon Machine Images (AMIs).

INCORRECT: "Containerization" is incorrect. Containers are packaged software that runs in a Docker image. Services such as Amazon ECS and Fargate can run Docker containers.

INCORRECT: "Workflow automation" is incorrect. Workflow automation is a process or orchestrating automated actions—this is associated with services such as Chef and Puppet or AWS OpsWorks.

Question 10 Answer: 4

Explanation:

Amazon Simple Notification Service (Amazon SNS) is a web service that makes it easy to set up, operate, and send notifications from the cloud. Amazon SNS is used for building and integrating loosely-coupled, distributed applications.

NOTE: Sometimes AWS will expand abbreviations in answers and other times, like with this question, you just get the abbreviation. Therefore, there's no workaround; you have to know your abbreviations!

CORRECT: "Amazon SNS" is the right answer.

INCORRECT: "Amazon EBS" is incorrect. Amazon Elastic Block Storage (EBS) provides storage volumes for EC2 instances.

INCORRECT: "Amazon EFS" is incorrect. Amazon Elastic File System (EFS) provides an NFS filesystem for usage by EC2 instances.

INCORRECT: "Amazon RDS" is incorrect. Amazon Relational Database Service (RDS) provides a managed relational database service.

Question 11 Answer: 2

Explanation:

EFS is a fully-managed service that makes it easy to set up and scale file storage in the Amazon Cloud. EFS filesystems are mounted using the NFS protocol (which is a file-level protocol).

Access to EFS file systems from on-premises servers can be enabled via Direct Connect or AWS VPN.

You mount an EFS file system on your on-premises Linux server using the standard Linux mount command for mounting a file system via the NFSv4.1 or NFSv5 protocol.

CORRECT: "Amazon EFS" is the right answer.

INCORRECT: "Amazon S3" is incorrect. Amazon S3 is an object-level, not a file-level storage system.

INCORRECT: "Amazon EBS" is incorrect. Amazon Elastic Block Storage (EBS) is block-level storage that can only be accessed by EC2 instances from the same AZ as the EBS volume.

INCORRECT: "Amazon Glacier" is incorrect. Amazon Glacier is an archiving solution that is accessed through S3.

Question 12 Answer: 1

Explanation:

AWS Lambda is a serverless compute service that runs your code in response to events and automatically manages the underlying compute resources for you.

Lambda runs your code on high-availability compute infrastructure and performs all the administration of the total resources, including server and operating system maintenance, capacity provisioning and automatic scaling, code and security patch deployment, and code monitoring and logging. All you need to do is supply the code.

CORRECT: "AWS Lambda" is the right answer.

INCORRECT: "Amazon EC2" is incorrect. With Amazon EC2, you must manage the instance and operating system.

INCORRECT: "AWS CodeDeploy" is incorrect. AWS CodeDeploy is a fully managed deployment service that automates software deployments to a variety of computing services such as Amazon EC2, AWS Lambda, and your on-premises servers.

INCORRECT: "Amazon EKS" is incorrect. Amazon ElasticContainerService for Kubernetes (Amazon EKS) is a managed service that makes it easy for you to run Kubernetes on AWS withoutneeding to stand up or maintain your own Kubernetes control plane

Question 13 Answer: D

OFFICIAL EXPLANATION:

Through a hybrid cloud, a company can retain control over an internally managed private cloud, while depending on the public cloud, when required. For example, during peak time, you can migrate a few applications to the public cloud. In cloud computing, the hybrid cloud refers to the use of both on-premises resources in addition to public cloud resources.

Question 14 Answer: D

OFFICIAL EXPLANATION:

Through a hybrid cloud, a company can retain control over an internally managed private cloud, while depending on the public cloud, when required. For example, during peak time, you can migrate a few applications to the public cloud. In cloud computing, the hybrid cloud refers to the use of both on-premises resources in addition to public cloud resources.

Question 15 Answer: A, C

OFFICIAL EXPLANATION:

Physical infrastructure is the responsibility of AWS and not with the customer. Hence it is not an advantage of moving to the AWS Cloud, And AWS provides security mechanisms. Still, even the responsibility of security lies with the customer.

Question 16 Answer: 4, 5

Explanation:

With infrastructure as code AWS assets are programmable, so you can apply techniques, practices, and tools from software development to make your whole infrastructure reusable, maintainable, extensible, and testable.

With bootstrapping, you can execute automated actions to modify default configurations. This includes scripts that install software or copy data to bring that resource to a particular state.

CORRECT: "Bootstrapping" is a right answer.

CORRECT: "Infrastructure as code" is also theright answer.

INCORRECT: "Snapshotting" is incorrect. Snapshotting is about saving data, not instantiating resources.

INCORRECT: "Fault tolerance" is incorrect. Fault tolerance is a method of increasing the availability of your system when components fail.

INCORRECT: "Performance monitoring" is incorrect. Performance monitoring has nothing to do with instantiating resources.

Question 17 Answer: 4

Explanation:

AWS allows customers to assign metadata to their AWS resources,in the form of tags. Each tag is a simple label consisting of a customer-defined key and an optional value that can make it easier to manage, search for, and filter resources. AWS Cost Explorer and detailed billing reports support the ability to break down AWS costs by tag.

The other options are incorrect as they are not methods of adding metadata to an AWS resource.

CORRECT: "Tagging" is the right answer.

INCORRECT: "Labelling" is incorrect as explained above.

INCORRECT: "Access Control" is incorrect as explained above.

INCORRECT: "Categorizing" is incorrect as explained above.

Question 18 Answer: 1

Explanation:

An Amazon Virtual Private Cloud (VPC) spans all availability zones within a region.

CORRECT: "Spans all Availability Zones within the region" is the right answer.

INCORRECT: "Spans all Availability Zones globally," is incorrect. VPCs do not span regions; you create VPCs in each region.

INCORRECT: "At least two subnets per region" is incorrect. VPCs are not limited by subnets, subnets are created within AZs, and you can have many subnets in an AZ

INCORRECT: "At least 2 data centers per region" is incorrect.

Question 19 Answer: 4

Explanation:

AWS CodeCommitis a fully-managed source control service that hosts secure Git-based repositories. It makes it easy for teams to collaborate on code in a secure and highly scalable ecosystem.

CORRECT: "AWS CodeCommit" is the right answer.

INCORRECT: "AWS CodeStar" isincorrect. AWS CodeStar enables you to develop, build, and deploy applications on AWS quickly. AWS CodeStarprovides a unified user interface, enabling you to easily manage your software development activities in one place.

INCORRECT: "AWS Cloud9" is incorrect. AWS Cloud9 is a cloud-based integrated development environment (IDE) that lets you write, run, and debug your code with just a browser.

INCORRECT: "AWS CodeDeploy" isincorrect. AWS CodeDeployis a deployment service that automates application deployments to Amazon EC2 instances, on-premisesinstances, or serverless Lambda functions.

Question 20 Answer: 4, 5

Explanation:

Elastic Web-Scale computing– you can increase or decrease capacity within minutes not hours and commission one to thousands of instances simultaneously.

Inexpensive – Amazon passes on the financial benefits of scale by chargingmeager rates and on a capacity consumed basis.

CORRECT: "Elastic web-scale computing" is a right answer.

CORRECT: "Inexpensive" is also theright answer.

INCORRECT: "High-availability with an SLA of 99.999%" is incorrect. AWS provide an SLA for EC2 that states that services will be available within each AWS region with a Monthly Uptime Percentage of at least 99.99%

INCORRECT: "Complete control of the hypervisor layer" is incorrect. Amazon EC2 does not provide any control of the hypervisor or underlying hardware infrastructure.

Question 21 Answer: 1

Explanation:

Amazon EC2 Auto Scaling automatically responds to demand by adding or removing EC2 instances to ensure the right amount of computing capacity is available at any time. This can help to automatically adjust the number of instances based on the load on your application.

CORRECT: "Amazon EC2 Auto Scaling" is the right answer.

INCORRECT: "AWS ElastiCache" is incorrect. AWS ElastiCacheprovidesin-memory cache and database services

INCORRECT: "Amazon Elastic Load Balancing" is incorrect. Amazon ELB distributes incoming requests to EC2 instances. It can be used in conjunction with Auto Scaling

INCORRECT: "Amazon DynamoDB" is incorrect. DynamoDB is a non-relational (NoSQL)

Question 22 Answer: 3

Explanation:

As application complexity increases, a desirable attribute of an IT system is that it can be broken into smaller, loosely coupled components. This means that IT systems should be designed in a way that reduces interdependencies—a change or a failure in one part should not cascade to other components

The concept of loose coupling includes "well-defined interfaces," which reduce interdependencies in a system by enabling interaction only through specific, technology-agnostic interfaces (e.g., RESTful APIs).

CORRECT: "Loose Coupling," is the right answer.

INCORRECT: "Services, Not Servers" is incorrect. This best practice encourages the use of a wider variety of AWS services in your application architectures.

INCORRECT: "Removing Single Points of Failure" is incorrect. This best practice aims to increase system availability.

INCORRECT: "Automation" is incorrect. This best practice encourages the use of automation for efficiency and consistency.

Question 23 Answer: 1

Explanation:

AWS CloudFormation provides a common language for you to describe and provision all the infrastructure resources in your cloud environment.

CloudFormation allows you to use a simple text file to model and provision, in an automated and secure manner, all the resources needed for your applications across all regions and accounts.

CORRECT: "AWS CloudFormation" is the right answer.

INCORRECT: "AWS Elastic Beanstalk" is incorrect. AWS Elastic Beanstalk is used for running applications in a managed environment. It is not used for deploying templated configurations.

INCORRECT: "AWS CodeBuild" is incorrect. AWS CodeBuild is a fully managed continuous integration service that compiles source code runs tests, and produces software packages that are ready to deploy.

INCORRECT: "AWS CodeDeploy" is incorrect. AWS CodeDeploy is a fully managed deployment service that automates software deployments to a variety of computing services such as Amazon EC2, AWS Lambda, and on-premises servers. It does not use a templated configuration for deployment.

Question 24 Answer: 4

Explanation:

Latency (slow response times) is experienced when resources are far away. Distance is the single biggest factor that causes latency. The easiest option presented to resolve this situation is to place resources closer to where the users are.

CORRECT: "Provision resources in the Asia Pacific (Sydney) Region in Australia" is the correct answer.

INCORRECT: "Implement AWS Direct Connect for users in Australia" is incorrect. Direct Connect is a private network connection from your network or data center into a nearby AWS Region. This does not solve the latency issues.

INCORRECT: "Use AWS Transit Gateway to quickly route users from Australia to the application" is incorrect. This service is used to connect Amazon Virtual Private Clouds (VPCs) and on-premises networks to a single gateway for connecting multiple VPCs and on-premises networks. This does not solve the latency issues.

INCORRECT: "Launch additional Amazon EC2 instances in Frankfurt to handle the demand" is incorrect. Latency will still be an issue even with more resources in Frankfurt.

Question 25 Correct Answer(s): 1

Explanation:

As application complexity increases, a desirable attribute of an IT system is that it can be broken into smaller, loosely coupled components.

This means that IT systems should be designed in a way that reduces interdependencies—a change or a failure in one component should not cascade to other parts.

CORRECT: "Implement loose coupling" is the right answer.

Security

Question 1 Correct Answer(s): 3, 4

Explanation:

Under the AWS shared responsibility model, AWS are responsible for security "of" the cloud and customers are responsible for security "in" the cloud. Securing data in transit and ensuring the integrity of data are customer responsibilities. Customers are always responsible for managing data including encryption.

CORRECT: "Security of data in transit" is a right answer.

CORRECT: "Data integrity authentication" is also a right answer.

Question 2 Correct Answer(s): B, E

Explanation:

"Inherited Controls are controls which a customer fully inherits from AWS such as physical controls and environmental controls.

For example: Let's say you have built an application in AWS for customers to store their data securely. But your customers are concerned about the security of the data and ensuring compliance requirements are met. To address this, you assure your customer that "our company does not host customer data in its corporate or remote offices, but rather in AWS data centers that have been certified to meet industry security standards."That includes physical and environmental controls to secure the data, which is the responsibility of Amazon. Companies do not have physical access to the AWS data centers. As such, they fully inherit the biological and environmental controls from AWS.

You can read more about AWS' data center controls here:

https://aws.amazon.com/compliance/data-center/controls/

Option A is not correct. Communications controls are the responsibility of the customer.

Options C & D are not correct. Patch Management and Configuration Management have shared controls.

Question 3 Correct Answer(s): 3

Explanation:

Identity and access management (IAM) Policies are documents that define permissions and can be applied to users, groups, and roles. IAM policies can be written to grant access to Amazon S3 buckets.

CORRECT: "IAM Policy" is the right answer.

Question 4 Correct Answer(s): 1, 3

Explanation:

AWS is responsible for the "security of the cloud." This includes protecting the infrastructure that runs all of the services offered in the AWS Cloud. This infrastructure is composed of the hardware, software, networking, and facilities that run AWS Cloud services.

The customer is responsible for "security in the cloud." Customer responsibility depends on the service consumed but includes aspects such as Identity and Access Management (includes password policies), encryption of data, protection of network traffic, and operating system, network and firewall configuration.

Question 5 Correct Answer(s): 3

Explanation:

The identity and access management service (IAM) is used to control individual and group access to AWS resources securely. IAM can also be used to manage multi-factor authentication (MFA). With MFA, you add an additional factor of authentication such as Google Authenticator device. This is "something you have" and is used with your password "something, you know."

CORRECT: "AWS IAM" is the right answer.

Question 6 Correct Answer(s): 3, 4

Explanation:

AWS is responsible for "Security of the Cloud" and customers are responsible for "Security in the Cloud."

AWS is responsible for items such as the physical security of the DC, replacement of old disk drives, and patch management of the infrastructure

Customers are responsible for items such as configuring security groups, network ACLs, patching their operating systems and encrypting their data

CORRECT: "Configuration of security groups" is a right answer.

CORRECT: "Encryption of customer data," is also theright answer.

Question 7 Correct Answer(s): 2, 3

Explanation:

AWS Key Management Service (KMS) gives you centralized control over the encryption keys used to protect your data. AWS CloudHSMis a cloud-based hardware security module (HSM) that enables you to easily generate and use your encryption keys on the AWS Cloud.

CORRECT: "AWS CloudHSM" is a right answer.

CORRECT: "AWS KMS" is also theright answer.

Question 8 Correct Answer(s): 2, 3

Explanation:

For extra security, AWS recommends that you require multi-factor authentication (MFA) for all users in your account. With MFA, users, have a device that generates a response to an authentication challenge.

Both the user's credentials (something you know) and the device-generated response (something you have) are required to complete the sign-in process. If a user's password or access keys are compromised, your account resources are still secure because of the additional authentication requirement.

Additionally, strong password policies should be used to enforce measures including minimum password length, complexity, and password reuse restrictions.

CORRECT: "AWS Multi-Factor Authentication (AWS MFA)" is a right answer.

CORRECT: "Strong password policies" is also theright answer.

Question 9 Correct Answer(s): 3

Explanation:

Inspector is an automated security assessment service that helps improve the security and compliance of applications deployed on

AWS. The Inspector automatically assesses applications for vulnerabilities or deviations from best practices.

CORRECT: "Use AWS Inspector" is the right answer.

Question 10 Correct Answer(s): 3

Explanation:

AWS Key Management Service gives you centralized control over the encryption keys used to protect your data. You can create, import, rotate, disable, delete, define usage policies for, and audit the use of encryption keys used to encrypt your data.

Note: Make sure you know your abbreviations! Sometimes AWS will expand them and other times they won't, it varies by question. Therefore, you must know the abbreviations for all services in scope for the exam.

CORRECT: "AWS KMS" is the right answer.

Question 11 Correct Answer(s): 4

Explanation:

AWS WAF is a web application firewall that protects against common exploits that could compromise application availability, compromise security or consume excessive resources.

CORRECT: "AWS WAF" is the right answer.

Question 12 Correct Answer(s): 1

Explanation:

Groups are collections of users and have policies attached to them. You can use groups to assign permissions to multiple users. To do this, place the users in the group and then create an IAM policy with the correct permissions and attach it to the group.

You do not use an IAM User, Role, or password policy to assign permissions to multiple users.

CORRECT: "IAM Group" is the right answer.

Question 13 Correct Answer(s): 3

Explanation:

With IAM Roles, you can delegate permissions to resources for users and services without using permanent credentials (e.g., username and password). To do so, you can create a role and assign an IAM policy to the part that has the permissions required.

CORRECT: "IAM Role" is the right answer.

Question 14 Correct Answer(s): 2

Explanation:

You cannot associate an access key ID and secret access key with an IAM Group, Role, or Policy.

CORRECT: "IAM User" is the right answer.

Question 15 Correct Answer(s): 3

Explanation:

AWS Config is a fully-managed service that provides you with an AWS resource inventory, configuration history, and configuration change notifications to enable security and regulatory compliance.

CORRECT: "Configure AWS Config with the resource types" is the right answer.

Question 16 Correct Answer(s): 2

Explanation:

AWS Artifact is the go-to, central resource for compliance-related information that matters to you. It provides on-demand access to AWS' security and compliance reports and select online agreements.

Reports available in AWS Artifact include Service Organization Control (SOC) reports, Payment Card Industry (PCI) reports, and certifications from accreditation bodies across geographies and compliance verticals that validate the implementation and operating effectiveness of AWS security controls.

CORRECT: "AWS Artifact" is the right answer.

Question 17 Answer: D

Explanation:

"Since you are going to create snapshots in another geographical location, then you will make them in another AWS Region.

Question 18 Answer: A

Explanation:

"Amazon Simple Storage Service (Amazon S3) is AWS' large, secure, and feature-rich object storage service

Question 19 Answer: C

Explanation:

"Customers should be aware that their responsibilities may vary depending on the AWS services chosen. For example, when using Amazon EC2, you are responsible for applying the operating system and application security patches regularly. However, such patches are applied automatically when using Amazon RDS.

Question 20 Answer: A

Explanation:

"RDS is the AWS's relational database service.

Question 21 Answer: A, D

Explanation:

"** Amazon EC2 Auto Scaling continually monitors the utilization of the instances underlying your application to make sure that your application always has the right amount of computing. In other words, Amazon EC2 Auto Scaling automatically scales the models up during demand spikes (to increase the availability of the application) or scales them down when demand lulls (to minimize costs).

Question 22 Answer: A, B

Explanation:

"AWS is continuously innovating the design and systems of its data centers to protect them from human-made and natural risks. For example, at the first layer of security, AWS provides several security features depending on the location, such as security guards, fencing, security feeds, intrusion detection technology, and other security measures.

According to the Shared Responsibility Model, Patching of the underlying hardware is the AWS's responsibility. AWS is responsible for patching and fixing flaws within the infrastructure. Still, customers are responsible for repairing their guest OS and applications.

Question 23 Answer: 1, 5

Explanation:

Both AWS KMS and AWS CloudHSM can be used to generate data encryption keys. You use what is called customer master keys (CMKs) to create data encryption keys. The data encryption keys can then be used actually to encrypt the data.

CORRECT: "AWS Key Management Service (AWS KMS)" is a right answer.

CORRECT: "AWS CIoudHSM" is also theright answer.

INCORRECT: "Amazon Macie" isincorrect. Amazon Macieis a fully managed data security and data privacy service that uses machine learning and pattern matching to discover and protect your sensitive data in AWS

INCORRECT: "AWS Certificate Manager" is incorrect. AWS Certificate Manager is a service that lets you easily provision, manage, and deploy public and private Secure Sockets Layer/Transport Layer Security (SSL/TLS) certificates for use with AWS services and your internal connected resources.

Technology

Question 1 Answer: 4, 5

Explanation:

Under the AWS shared responsibility model, AWS is responsible for security "of" the cloud, and customers are responsible for security "in" the cloud. Securing data in transit and ensuring the integrity of data are customer responsibilities. Customers are always responsible for managing data, including encryption.

CORRECT: "Security of data in transit" is the right answer.

CORRECT: "Data integrity authentication" is also the right answer.

INCORRECT: "Physical and environmental security" is wrong as this is security "of" the cloud and, therefore, the responsibility of AWS.

INCORRECT: "Physical network devices including firewalls" are wrong as this is security "of" the cloud and, therefore, the responsibility of AWS.

INCORRECT: "Storage device decommissioning" is incorrect as this is security "of" the cloud and, therefore, the responsibility of AWS.

Question 2 Answer: 4

Explanation:

For maximum redundancy and fault tolerance, the application should be deployed in multiple AWS Regions and multiple Availability Zones within each of those regions. This architecture may use Elastic Load Balancers and Amazon Route 53 records to direct traffic to instances. Alternatively, it could use AWS Global Accelerator.

CORRECT: "Across multiple Availability Zones in two AWS Regions" is the right answer.

INCORRECT: "In a single Availability Zone in one AWS Region" is erroneous as this does not represent the highest redundancy and fault tolerance.

INCORRECT: "In a single Availability Zone in two AWS Regions" is erroneous as this does not represent the highest redundancy and fault tolerance.

INCORRECT: "Across multiple Availability Zones in one AWS Region" is erroneous as this does not represent the highest redundancy and fault tolerance.

Question 3 Answer: 3

Explanation:

Elasticity means that your infrastructure scales based on actual usage. When you have higher demand, you use more infrastructure and pay more, and when you have less request, you need less infrastructure and pay less. The benefits are you don't need to guess about capacity and pay only for what you need.

CORRECT: "Elasticity of the AWS Cloud" is the right answer.

INCORRECT: "Easy global deployments" is erroneous. It is easy to deploy many AWS resources globally. Still, this benefit does not eliminate the need to estimate future usage.

INCORRECT: "Security of the AWS Cloud" is erroneous. The security of the AWS Cloud is essential but does not eliminate the need to estimate future usage.

INCORRECT: "Economies of scale" is erroneous. It means you pay less for some resources because of the benefits of AWS's scale. However, this benefit does not eliminate the need to estimate future usage.

Question 4 Answer: 1, 4

Explanation:

An AWS Managed VPN is a virtual private network connection over the public Internet. It creates an encrypted link between the on-premises network and your AWS VPC.

CORRECT: "AWS Managed VPN" is the right answer.

CORRECT: "AWS Direct Connect" is also the right answer.

Question 5 Answer: 4

Explanation:

You can back up the data on your Amazon EBS volumes to Amazon S3 by taking point-in-time snapshots.

Question 6 Answer: 2

Explanation:

Latency (slow response times) is experienced when resources are far away. Distance is the single most significant factor that causes latency. The easiest option presented to resolve this situation is to place resources closer to where the users are.

CORRECT: "Provision resources in the Asia Pacific (Sydney) Region in Australia" is the right answer.

INCORRECT: "Implement AWS Direct Connect for users in Australia" is erroneous. Direct Connect is a private network connection from your network or data center into a nearby AWS Region. It does not solve the latency issues.

INCORRECT: "Use AWS Transit Gateway to route users from Australia to the application" quickly is wrong. This service is used to connect Amazon Virtual Private Clouds (VPCs) and on-premises networks to a single gateway for connecting multiple VPCs and on-premises systems. It does not solve the latency issues.

INCORRECT: "Launch additional Amazon EC2 instances in Frankfurt to handle the demand" is erroneous. Latency will still be an issue even with more resources in Frankfurt.

Question 7Answer: 4

Explanation:

Only the enterprise plan provides Well-Architected Reviews and Operational Reviews. 24/7 access to Cloud Support Engineers through email, online chat, and the phone is offered on the business and enterprise plans.

CORRECT: "Enterprise" is the right answer.

INCORRECT: "Basic" is erroneous. Basic only includes 24x7 access to customer service, documentation, whitepapers, and support forums.

INCORRECT: "Business" is wrong as it does not provide access to architectural and operational reviews.

INCORRECT: "Developer" is erroneous as you get support from Cloud Support Associates, not Engineers, and also do not get access to architectural and operational reviews.

Question 8 Answer: 2, 4

Explanation:

A couple of the benefits that companies will realize immediately when using the AWS Cloud have increased agility and a change from capital expenditure to variable operational spending.

Agility is enabled through the flexibility of cloud services and the ease with which applications can be deployed, scaled, and managed. When using cloud services, you pay for what you use, and this is a variable, operational expense that can be beneficial to company cashflow.

CORRECT: "Capital expenses are replaced with variable expenses" is theright answer.

CORRECT: "Increased agility" is also theright answer.

INCORRECT: "Variable expenses are replaced with capital expenses" is incorrect. It is the wrong way around; capital expenses are replaced with variable costs.

INCORRECT: "User control of physical infrastructure" is incorrect. It is not true; you do not get control of the physical infrastructure.

Question 9 Answer: 1, 3

Explanation:

Edge Locations are parts of the Amazon CloudFront content delivery network (CDN) that are all around the world and are used to get content closer to end-users for better performance.

AWS Shield, which protects against Distributed Denial of Service (DDoS) attacks, is available globally on Amazon CloudFront Edge Locations.

CORRECT: "Amazon CloudFront" is theright answer.

CORRECT: "AWS Shield" is also theright answer.

INCORRECT: "AWS Direct Connect" is erroneous. AWS Direct Connect is a networking service used for creating a hybrid cloud between on-premises and AWS Cloud using a private network connection

INCORRECT: "Amazon EBS" is erroneous. Amazon EBS is a storage service.

INCORRECT: "AWS Config" is erroneous. AWS Config is used for evaluating the configuration state of AWS resources.

Question 10 Answer: 1

Explanation:

When you deploy an application across multiple Availability Zones, the application can be considered to be highly available. You must also have a way of directing traffic to the application in each AZ, such as an Elastic Load Balancer.

CORRECT: "Being highly available" is the right answer.

INCORRECT: "Having global reach" is incorrect as this refers to deploying applications that can be connected to from around the world and also deploying applications into different regions.

INCORRECT: "Being secure" is incorrect as this is not an example of the implementation of security.

INCORRECT: "Having elasticity" is erroneous. Auto Scaling is an example of elasticity, and it is not mentioned in this question.

Question 11 Answer: 1, 3

Explanation:

AWS Elastic Beanstalk and AWS CloudFormation are both examples of automation. Beanstalk is a platform service that leverages the automation capabilities of CloudFormation to build out application architectures.

CORRECT: "AWS Elastic Beanstalk" is theright answer.

CORRECT: "AWS CloudFormation" is also theright answer.

INCORRECT: "Elastic Load Balancing" is erroneous. Elastic Load Balancing (ELB) is used for distributing incoming connections to Amazon EC2 instances. It is not an example of automation; it is load balancing.

INCORRECT: "Amazon Elastic File System (EFS)" is wrong. Amazon EFS is a file system.

INCORRECT: "AWS Lambda" is erroneous. AWS Lambda is a computing service, not an automation service.

Question 12 Answer: 4

Explanation:

The Business support plan provides a service level agreement (SLA) of < 1 hour for production system down support cases.

CORRECT: "Open a production system down support case" is the right answer.

INCORRECT: "Contact the dedicated Technical Account Manager" is incorrect. The dedicated TAM only comes with the Enterprise support plan.

INCORRECT: "Contact the dedicated AWS Concierge Support team" is incorrect. The concierge support team only comes with the Enterprise support plan.

INCORRECT: "Open a business-critical system down support case" is incorrect. The business-critical system down support only comes with the Enterprise support plan.

Question 13 Answer: 2

Explanation:

Elasticity refers to the automatic scaling of resources based on demand. The benefit is that you provide only the necessary resources at a given time (optimizing cost) and don't have to worry about absorbing spikes in demand.

CORRECT: "By automatically scaling resources based on demand," is the right answer.

INCORRECT: "By reducing interdependencies between application components" is incorrect. Elasticity does not reduce interdependencies between systems – this is known as loose coupling.

INCORRECT: "By selecting the correct storage tier for your workload," is incorrect. Selecting the correct storage tier would be an example of right-sizing, not elasticity.

INCORRECT: "By reserving capacity to reduce cost" is incorrect. Reserving capacity to reduce cost refers to using reservations such as EC2 Reserved Instances.

Question 14 Answer:

Explanation:

Question 15 Answer: 1

Explanation:

An Amazon Virtual Private Cloud (VPC) spans all availability zones within a region.

CORRECT: "Spans all Availability Zones within the region" is the right answer.

Question 16 Answer: 1

Explanation:

AWS Shield Advanced provides enhanced detection and includes a specialized support team for customers on Enterprise or Business support plans. The AWS DDoS Response Team (DRT) is available 24/7 and can be engaged before, during, or after a DDoS attack.

CORRECT: "AWS Shield Advanced" is the right answer.

INCORRECT: "AWS Firewall Manager" is erroneous. This service is used to simplify the management of AWS WAF, AWS Shield Advanced, and Amazon VPC security groups.

INCORRECT: "AWS Web Application Firewall" is incorrect. AWS WAF is used for protecting web applications and APIs against malicious attacks. It is not a DDoS prevention service.

INCORRECT: "Amazon GuardDuty" is incorrect. This service is used for continuously monitoring AWS resources for threats. It is not a DDoS prevention service; it uses machine learning and anomaly detection to identify security vulnerabilities in resources.

Question 17 Answer: 4

Explanation:

A Network ACL is a firewall that is associated with a subnet within your VPC. It is used to filter the network traffic that enters and exits the subnet.

CORRECT: "Network Access Control List" is the right answer.

INCORRECT: "IAM Policy" is incorrect. An IAM policy is used to assign permissions to users and roles.

INCORRECT: "Bucket Policy" is incorrect. A Bucket Policy is used with Amazon S3 buckets to control access.

Question 18 Answer: 3, 5

Explanation:

Recovery procedures should always be tested ahead of any outage of a disaster recovery situation.

When designing systems, it is also an excellent practice to implement automatic recovery when possible. It reduces or eliminates the operational burden and potential downtime associated with a failure of a system or application component.

CORRECT: "Testing recovery procedures" is the right answer.

CORRECT: "Automatically recovering from failure" is the right answer.

INCORRECT: "Using monolithic architecture" is incorrect. A monolithic architecture means you have multiple components of an application running on a single system. It results in a more significant issue if that system fails. A distributed architecture is preferred.

INCORRECT: "Measuring overall efficiency" is incorrect. Efficiency has more of a bearing on cost management than reliability.

INCORRECT: "Adopting a consumption model" is wrong. A consumption model has benefits more aligned with cost and agility than reliability.

Question 19 Answer: 1, 5

Explanation:

Subnets and Security groups can be configured from within the VPC console.

CORRECT: "Subnets" is the right answer.

CORRECT: "Security Groups" is the right answer.

Question 20 Answer: 2, 3

Explanation:

IAM groups are used for organizing users and applying policies (permissions) to them. You can add users to multiple groups. Groups cannot be nested, which means you cannot have a group as a member of another group or organize groups in a hierarchy.

CORRECT: "A user can be a member of multiple groups" is theright answer.

CORRECT: "Groups can contain users only and cannot be nested" is also theright answer.

INCORRECT: "Groups can be nested and can contain other groups" is erroneous. You cannot make a group a member of another group or organize them in a hierarchy.

INCORRECT: "A user can only be a member of a single group at one a time" is wrong. It is not true; users can be members of multiple groups.

INCORRECT: "All new users are automatically added to a default group" is erroneous. There is no default group that users are added to when they are created.

Question 21 Answer: 1, 3

Explanation:

You may choose a region to reduce latency, minimize costs, or address regulatory requirements.

Latency is the delay caused mostly by distance. It means you should choose to create your buckets in Regions that are closer (physically) to your users.

Some countries or industries have regulations that mandate data must not leave a jurisdiction or country border. In this case, you simply select an AWS Region accordingly.

Question 22 Answer: 4

Explanation:

Auto Scaling allows the dynamic adjustment of provisioned resources based on demand. For instance, you can use Amazon EC2 Auto Scaling to launch additional EC2 models when CloudWatch metrics report the CPU utilization has reached a certain threshold.

CORRECT: "Auto Scaling" is the right answer.

Question 23 Answer: 3

Explanation:

AWS is responsible for updating Amazon EC2 host firmware. It is considered "security of the cloud." All other tasks are the responsibility of the customer.

CORRECT: "Updating Amazon EC2 host firmware" is the right answer.

INCORRECT: "Granting access to individuals and services" is erroneous. It is something a customer must perform to control access to the resources they use on AWS.

INCORRECT: "Encrypting data in transit" is incorrect. Encryption at rest and in-transit is a customer responsibility.

INCORRECT: "Updating operating systems" is incorrect. Customers are responsible for patching operating systems on Amazon EC2. AWS is only responsible for the host servers.

Question 24 Answer: 3

Explanation:

An Amazon Elastic Block Store (EBS) volume is often described as a "virtual hard disk in the cloud."

CORRECT: "Amazon EBS volume" is the right answer.

INCORRECT: "Amazon EFS Filesystem" is incorrect. An Amazon EFS filesystem is a file-level storage system that is accessed using the NFS protocol. Filesystems are mounted at the file, rather than the block level and are therefore not similar to a virtual hard disk.

INCORRECT: "Amazon S3 Bucket" is incorrect. Amazon S3 is an object-level storage service and is not mounted or attached. You use a REST API over HTTPS to access objects in an object-store.

INCORRECT: "Amazon ENI" is incorrect. An Amazon Elastic Network Interface is a networking construct, not a storage construct.

Question 25 Answer: 3

Explanation:

Amazon EC2 Auto Scaling scales horizontally by adding launching and terminating EC2 instances based on actual demand for your application.

CORRECT: "Horizontal" is the right answer.

INCORRECT: "Vertical" is incorrect as EC2 auto-scaling scales horizontally.

INCORRECT: "Linear" is incorrect as this is not the way Auto Scaling works.

INCORRECT: "Incremental" is incorrect as this is not the way Auto Scaling works.

Billing and Pricing

Question 1 Answer: B

OFFICIAL EXPLANATION:

AWS Secrets Manager is integrated with AWS CloudTrail. This service provides a record of actions taken by a user, role, or an AWS service in Secrets Manager. CloudTrail captures all API calls for Secrets Manager as events, including calls from the Secrets Manager console and code calls to the Secrets Manager APIs.

Question 2 Answer: A, C, D

OFFICIAL EXPLANATION:

The responsibility of AWS includes the following 1) Securing edge locations, 2) Monitoring physical device security, 3) Implementing service organization Control (SOC) standards

Question 3 Answer: A

OFFICIAL EXPLANATION:

The AWS team undertakes the critical measure for providing non-stop monitoring, logging, and auditing of physical access controls.

Question 4 Answer: D

OFFICIAL EXPLANATION:

Through a hybrid cloud, a company can retain control over an internally managed private cloud, while depending on the public cloud, when required. For example, during peak time, you can migrate a few applications to the public cloud.

Question 5 Answer: C

OFFICIAL EXPLANATION:

Provisioned IOPS is used for applications and databases where there is a significant amount of traffic. **Question 6 Answer: C**

OFFICIAL EXPLANATION:

The attributes are also called columns or fields.

Question 7 Answer: D

OFFICIAL EXPLANATION:

AWS Region is another vital feature of the Navigation Bar. If a service supports Regions, the resources in each Region are independent. For example, if you create an Amazon EC2 instance or an Amazon SQS queue in one Region, the model or column is independent of instances or queues in another Region.

Question 8 Answer: C

OFFICIAL EXPLANATION:

Other enterprise applications like databases or ERP systems often require dedicated, low latency storage for each host. This is analogous to direct-attached storage (DAS) or a Storage Area Network (SAN). Block-based cloud storage solutions like Amazon Elastic Block Store (EBS) are provisioned with each virtual server and offer the ultra-low latency required for high-performance workloads.

Question 9 Answer: E

OFFICIAL EXPLANATION:

Screenshot in AWS Doc shows what services the Trusted Advisor Dashboard offers.

Question 10 Answer: B

OFFICIAL EXPLANATION:

The AWS Documentation mentions the following Amazon Simple Notification Service (Amazon SNS) is a web service that enables applications, end-users, and devices to send and receive notifications from the cloud instantly.

Question 11 Answer: D

OFFICIAL EXPLANATION:

Through a hybrid cloud, a company can retain control over an internally managed private cloud, while depending on the public cloud, when required. For example, during peak time, you can migrate a few applications to the public cloud.

Question 12 Answer: C

OFFICIAL EXPLANATION:

Users can access Amazon Web Services through Management Console, Command Line Interface, Command Line Tools, AWS Software Development Kits, and Query APIs.

Question 13 Answer: C

OFFICIAL EXPLANATION:

The C3 instance type offers high-frequency processors for enhanced networking, clustering, and instance storage.

Question 14 Answer: D

OFFICIAL EXPLANATION:

Quickly launch the replacement compute capacity in the cloud for business continuity. After the disaster, restore your data to the data center and terminate the EC2 instances.

Question 15 Answer: C,D

OFFICIAL EXPLANATION:

As per the Shared Responsibility Model, the security for users has to be managed by the AWS Customer.

Question 16 Answer: C

OFFICIAL EXPLANATION:

Since EC2 Instances carry a charge when they are running, you need to factor in the number of servers that need to be migrated to AWS.

Question 17 Answer: A and B

OFFICIAL EXPLANATION:

Full Trusted Advisor Benefits

Business Support and Enterprise Support customers get access to the full set of Trusted Advisor checks and recommendations. It helps optimize your entire AWS infrastructure, increase security and performance, reduce your overall costs, and monitor service limits. Additional benefits include:

Notifications: Stay up-to-date with your AWS resource deployment with weekly updates, plus create alerts and automate actions with Amazon CloudWatch.

Programmatic access: Retrieve and refresh Trusted Advisor results programmatically using AWS Support API.

Question 18 Answer: D

OFFICIAL EXPLANATION:

AWS Lambda service implements the code from Amazon EC2 instances on the virtual servers, in response to a triggered event.

Question 19 Answer: A

OFFICIAL EXPLANATION:

Amazon Route 53, a DNS Web service, is scalable, highly available, and a cost-effective medium to direct the visitors to a website, a virtual server, or a load balancer.

Question 20 Answer: A

OFFICIAL EXPLANATION:

A Load Balancer is responsible for distributing the network traffic across Amazon EC2 instances in different Availability Zones, which enables you to accomplish a higher fault-tolerance level.

Question 21 Answer: D

OFFICIAL EXPLANATION:
AWS Storage Gateway is a scalable and economic amalgamation of your office IT and AWS storage infrastructure.

Question 22 Answer: A

OFFICIAL EXPLANATION:

The disk was the first service offered by Amazon to transfer data using UPS or mail.

Question 23 Answer: B

Question 24 Answer: D

OFFICIAL EXPLANATION:

Designated Technical Account Manager (TAM) to proactively monitor your environment and assist with optimization.

Question 25 Answer: B

OFFICIAL EXPLANATION:

Storing thumbnails & transcoded media is one of the excellent use cases for storing content in AWS RRS, which can be used for later use.

CPSIA information can be obtained
at www.ICGtesting.com
Printed in the USA
LVHW082321220221
679697LV00023B/931